THE CA

THE CLASSIC GUIDE OF CABIN-LIFE
ON THE WATER BY BUILDING, FURNISHING,
AND MAINTAINING RUSTIC HOUSE BOATS

BY **RAYMOND S. SPEARS**

ORIGINALLY PUBLISHED IN 1913

LEGACY EDITION

CABIN LIFE AND CABIN CRAFT COLLECTION
BOOK 5

FEATURING

REMASTERED CLASSIC WORKS OF THE HIGHEST

QUALITY FROM **THE TIMELESS MASTERS AND**

TEACHERS OF TRADITIONAL HANDCRAFTS AND

OUTDOORS SKILLS

Doublebit Press
Eugene. OR

INTRODUCTION
To The Doublebit Press Legacy Edition

The old experts of the woods, mountains, and farm country life taught timeless principles and skills for decades. Through their books, the old experts offered rich descriptions of the outdoor world and encouraged learning through personal experiences in nature. Over the last 125 years, handcrafts, artisanal works, outdoors activities, and our experiences with nature have substantially changed. Many things have gotten simpler as equipment and processes have improved, and life outside, on the farm, or on the trail now brings with it many of the same comforts enjoyed in town. In addition, some activities of the old days are now no longer in vogue, or are even outright considered inappropriate or illegal. However, despite many of the positive changes in handcrafting, traditional skills, and outdoors methods that have occurred over the years, *there are many other skills and much knowledge that are at risk of being lost* that should never be forgotten.

By publishing Legacy Editions of classic texts on handcrafts, artisanal skills, nature lore, survival, and outdoors and camping life, it is our goal at Doublebit Press to do what we can to preserve and share the works from forgotten teachers that form the cornerstone of the authentic and hard-wrought American tradition of self-sustainability and self-reliance. Through remastered reprint editions of timeless classics of traditional crafts, classic methods, and outdoor recreation, perhaps we can regain some of this lost knowledge for future generations.

On the frontier, folks made virtually everything by hand. Old farmers' knowledge and homestead skills were passed on to the future generation because it meant survival. In addition, much of traditional handcrafts and outdoors life knowledge was passed on from American Indians – the original handcrafters and outdoorsmen of the Americas.

Today, much of the handcrafted items of the frontier are made in factories, only briefly seeing a human during the process (if at all). Making things by hand indeed takes much (often strenuous) work, but it provides an extreme sense of pride in the finished job. Instantly, all hand-made items come with a story on their creation. Most importantly, though, making items with traditional methods gives you experience and knowledge of how things work.

This is similar to the case of camping and the modern outdoors experience, with neatly arranged campsites at public campgrounds and camping gear that has been meticulously improved and tested in both the lab and the field. These changes have also caused us to lose this traditional knowledge, having it buried in the latest high-tech iteration of your latest camp gadget.

Many modern conveniences are only a brief trek away, with many parks, campgrounds, and even forests having easy-access roads, convenience stores, and even cell phone signal. In some ways, it is much easier to camp and go outdoors today, and that is a good thing! We should not be miserable when we go outside — lovers of the outdoors know the essential restorative capability that the woods can have on the body, mind, and soul. But to experience it, you need to not be surrounded by modern high-tech robotic coffee pots, tents that build themselves, or watches that tell you how to do everything!

Although things have gotten easier on us in the 21st Century when it comes to handcrafts and the outdoors, it certainly does not mean that we should forget the foundations of technical skills, artisanal production, and outdoors lore. All of the modern tools and cool gizmos that make our lives easier are all founded on principles of traditional methods that the old masters knew well and taught to those who would listen. We just have to look deeply into the design of our modern gadgets and factories to see the original methods and traditional skills at play.

Every woods master and artisan had their own curriculum or thought some things were more important than others. The old masters also taught common things in slightly different ways or did things differently than others. That's what makes each of the experts different and worth reading. There's no universal way of doing something, especially today. Learning to go about something differently helps with mastery or learn a new skill altogether. Basically, you learn intimately how things work, giving you great skill with adapting and being flexible when the need arises.

Again, to use the metaphor from the above paragraphs, traditional skills mastery consists of learning the basic building blocks of how and why the old artisans made things, how they lived outdoors, and why woods and nature lore mattered. Everything is intertwined, and doing it by hand increases your knowledge of this complex network. Each master goes about describing these building blocks differently or shows a different aspect of them.

Therefore, we have decided to publish this Legacy Edition reprint in our collection of traditional handcraft and outdoors life classics. This book is an important contribution to the early American traditional skills and outdoors literature, and has important historical and collector value toward preserving the American tradition of self-sufficiency and artisan production. The knowledge it holds is an invaluable reference for practicing outdoors skills and hand craft methods. Its chapters thoroughly discuss some of the essential building blocks of knowledge that are fundamental but may have been forgotten as equipment gets fancier and technology gets smarter. In short, this book was chosen for Legacy Edition printing because much of the basic skills and knowledge it contains has been forgotten or put to the wayside in trade for more modern conveniences and methods.

Although the editors at Doublebit Press are thrilled to have comfortable experiences in the woods and love our modern equipment for making cool hand-made projects, we are also realizing that the basic skills taught by the old masters are more essential than ever as our culture becomes more and more hooked on digital stuff. We don't want to risk forgetting the important steps, skills, or building blocks involved with each step of traditional methods. Sometimes, *there's no substitute for just doing something on your own, by hand.* Sometimes, to truly learn something is to *just do it by hand.* The Legacy Edition series represents the essential contributions to the American handcraft and outdoors tradition by the great experts.

With technology playing a major role in everyday life, sometimes we need to take a step back in time to find those basic building blocks used for gaining mastery – the things that we have luckily not completely lost and has been recorded in books over the last two centuries. These skills aren't forgotten, they've just been shelved. *It's time to unshelve them once again and reclaim the lost knowledge of self-sufficiency.*

Based on this commitment to preserving our outdoors and handcraft heritage, we have taken great pride in publishing this book as a complete original work without any editorial changes or revisions. We hope it is worthy of both study and collection by handcrafters and outdoors folk in the modern era and to fulfill its status as a Legacy Edition by passing along to the libraries of future generations.

Unlike many other low-resolution photocopy reproductions of classic books that are common on the market, this Legacy Edition does not simply place poor photography of old texts on our pages and use error-prone optical scanning or computer-generated text. We want our work to speak for itself and reflect the quality demanded by our customers who spend their hard-earned money. With this in mind, each Legacy Edition book that has been chosen for publication is carefully remastered from original print books, *with the Doublebit Legacy Edition printed and laid out in the exact way that it was presented at its original publication.* Our Legacy Edition books are inspired by the original covers of first-edition texts, embracing the beauty that is in both the simplicity and sometimes ornate decoration of vintage and antique books. We want provide a beautiful, memorable experience that is as true to the original text as best as possible, but with the aid of modern technology to make as meaningful a reading experience as possible for books that are typically over a century old.

Because of its age and because it is presented in its original form, the book may contain misspellings, inking errors, and other print blemishes that were common for the age. However, these are exactly the things that we feel give the book its character, which we preserved in this Legacy Edition. During digitization, we did our best to ensure that each illustration in the text was clean and sharp with the least amount of loss from being copied and digitized as possible. Full-page plate illustrations are presented as they were found, often including the extra blank page that was often behind a plate and plate pagination. For the covers, we use the original cover design as our template to give the book its original feel. We are sure you'll appreciate the fine touches and attention to detail that your Legacy Edition has to offer.

For traditional handcrafters and outdoors enthusiasts who demand the best from their equipment, this Doublebit Press Legacy Edition reprint was made with you in mind. Both important and minor details have equally both been accounted for by our publishing staff, down to the cover, font, layout, and images. It is the goal of Doublebit Legacy Edition series to preserve America's handcrafting and outdoors heritage, but also be cherished as collectible pieces, worthy of collection in any person's library and that can be passed to future generations.

Every book selected to be in this series offers unique views and instruction on important skills, advice, tips, tidbits, anecdotes, stories, and experiences that will enrichen the repertoire of any person looking to learn the skills it contains. To learn the most basic building blocks leads to mastery of all its aspects.

Studying This Book

The pages within this book present an overwhelming amount of information, facts, and directions to memorize that are often outdated and at the least, out of practice by modern standards. That doesn't mean that these pages have nothing to teach! It's just going to likely be new stuff for many readers.

Our one suggestion is *don't try to memorize everything,* especially when you're thumbing through the book or even reading it cover-to-cover. Many of our Legacy Edition books are antique or vintage. These writings from the late 1800's to early 1900's can be dense and out of style for someone not used to reading these types of books. Instead, gain some basic familiarity with each topic by thumbing through the pages, looking at the illustrations, and seeing the section headers. Then, choose a few topics or skills for deeper study.

Before you start a crafting project, or before camping or other outdoors trips can even begin, some planning and reflection is useful. First, it might be helpful to read through the book with plans in mind. The book can provide useful material for close study and reflection before you acquire equipment or head out to the field to practice.

Secondly, once you've come up with a practice plan, you will of course want to start doing tasks and skills. Doublebit Legacy Edition reprints all represent *learning by doing*, with each book containing many skills to master that have long sense been out of practice. But this is exactly why we print these books – these skills and methods should not be forgotten!

Any of the old artisans and tutors of woodcraft will tell you in their classic books that you can only truly learn how do stuff by *actually doing it*. Home study indeed does you well by using the many guidebooks that have been published over the previous 125 years. However, hundreds more lessons will become immediately available to you the moment you start with some of the old-style tasks.

For instance, before the days of camping outfitters, outdoors adventurers made their gear, which was tailored to their individual needs. Many experiments were done in the field to tweak their gear to get that ever-changing point of "perfect." Aside from experiencing wonderful lessons in history, getting outside and doing some of the activities this book will give you an appreciation for modern advances in outdoors and handcraft method and tools of the trade, as well as a deeper understanding of the foundations of outdoors and hand-craft life in the event that your gear fails you or you otherwise find yourself in situations where knowing the principles will get you unstuck fast.

If we were to tally up each of the individual tips in the Doublebit Library of Legacy Edition reprints, they would easily number in the thousands. The old masters represent centuries of previous knowledge that have been all but lost to 21st Century, technology-driven folks. To this point, although experience and *actually doing stuff* are the best forms of learning, taking a mindful approach to study of these works also benefit your development as a competent outdoorsperson and handcrafter.

You may also find it invaluable to take these volumes with you on your camping or other outdoors trips. In addition to having reading material on a variety of topics in the field for down time, you'll also find a thousand things to try in these pages if you're bored. Although skills may be best studied when in the field through experience and reflection, you may also study woods skills at home as well. Gaining familiarity through reading, videos, and other media are a great start toward building your ability toward gaining mastery in the field.

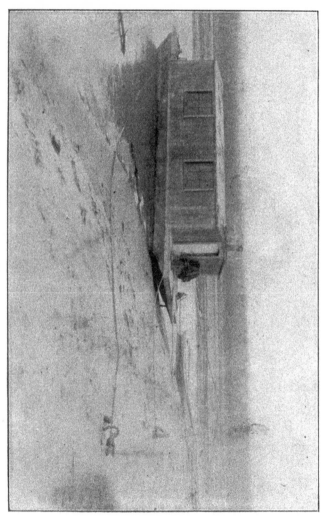

A Mississippi Shanty Boat.

The Cabin Boat Primer

Containing Descriptions and Diagrams, Photographs and Chapters on the Construction, Navigation and Use of House-Boats for Pleasure and Profit

Written and Compiled by

RAYMOND S. SPEARS

Published by

A. R. HARDING
Columbus, Ohio

INTRODUCTION

T HIS little book, The Cabin-boat Primer, is a compilation of facts and observations made by the author and compiler on a skiff and shanty-boat journey down the Mississippi river in 1903-4. In addition to these facts are descriptions as noted in the text, from the observations and experiences of others.

There are two narratives of trips on rivers added to the text of the Primer. These narratives give better than mere statements of. "How to do things," what the river shanty-boat and small boat traveler may expect when he goes afloat in wild or tame waters. Reading the fact articles and the chapters on cabin-boats, what to take and how to do things will clear the way for the would-be house-boater; but it is for the one who goes in a house-boat to keep his own eyes open for the unusual and the unexpected.

Things never happen twice exactly alike. There is always some little thing that requires ingenuity on the spot and at the time—ropes are tied thus and so, but when the rope breaks an entirely new condition arises to be met, and what to do when the rope breaks depends on the circumstances. Then is when people need their wits about them.

CONTENTS

ILLUSTRATIONS

CHAPTER I.

O N November 23, 1894, at 11 p. m., found Jim, John and George Wood and the scribe in Cairo, Illinois. Destination, down the river, no particular place, in search of game of any kind, but our aim was to find deer. A day later another person arrived who was to be one of our party in the person of Wat Hays whom we met at the depot.

We looked around Cairo to buy a cabin-boat and skiffs, Saturday, but found no cabinboat to suit us, then Jim Wood and I went across the Ohio River opposite Cairo and bought a John-boat—a flat-bottom boat about three and one-half feet wide by fourteen feet long—for $2.00, I think.

It was not much of a craft, as it leaked badly on account of being calked with old rope, beeswax and tallow, but thought it would do, and then we bought a pretty fair skiff for $4.00. We took these back across the river and tied them up near the Singer sawmill.

The next day being Sunday we hired a team at a livery stable and in company with a man that we knew who worked at the Singer sawmill, drove up to Mound City on the Ohio River in search of a cabin-boat—Jim, George, John, the man and I. We soon found one and bought it, paying $75.00 for it. George and I and the man we bought it of cut her loose and

(13)

floated down to Cairo while the rest came back in the rig we went up in.

We tied the cabin-boat up near the sawmill and the man unloaded his stuff on the bank, which consisted of stove, bed and bedding, a sinking machine, two mauls, a lot of pieces of old umbrellas, a grindstone and, as they say on a public farm sale bill, "a good many other articles too numerous to mention." Then we began to carry our things in—a cook stove, heating stove, five trunks, five cases of shotgun shells, a lot of flour, sugar, potatoes, etc., and a lot of cooking utensils and in fact everything necessary even to a two-gallon jug of snake medicine for several in town told us that the snakes were bad down the river in the canebrakes.

I forgot to give a little description of our cabin-boat, but the reader can form a better idea of it by looking at the picture. The cabin-boat was 40 or 45 feet long by 12 feet wide and the hull extended out over each end of the cabin and left a few feet of porch at each end. The gunnels were of 3-inch oak and the floor in the hull of 2-inch oak. The sides of the cabin were of ⅝-inch pine ceiling grooved and the cabin extended down in the hull. There was about a foot of space between the floor and bottom of the boat. The cabin was divided off into three rooms and at one end there was a pump to pump the water out of the hold in case she sprang a leak.

Our guns consisted of a rifle and a shotgun apiece. Our rifles were of various calibers; our shotguns were double barrels and pumps.

November 26th we passed our first night in the cabin-boat. We opened up our cots and set them around in the middle room, got our quilts and blankets out of our trunks and got ready to go to bed. Of

The Cabin Boat we Started With on our Trip.

course we stayed up late talking of the deer, turkey and other game we intended to kill on the trip, and it was after twelve before all got in bed.

It seemed the next morning that none of us were in a hurry to get up and when we did the sun had been up for some time. After breakfast Jim, John and I went up town to get a few things we needed and a few things we thought we needed before starting, and it was about two or three o'clock in the afternoon before we pulled out from the shore of the Ohio at Cairo.

We thought we could manage that big boat by tying a skiff in front and pulling on the oars, but we soon found out that we had run up against a big circumstance. I got in the skiff and we started. We went pretty well until we struck the current down by the wharf where the current carried us up against the shores, and the current was pretty swift. There was a big coal barge there and in it were a lot of coal heavers. Well, I saw we were going to hit it, and pretty hard at that, so I yelled to the coal heavers to ease us off. A big burly Irish coal heaver yelled:

"Let them go! They are only A. P. A.'s anyway."

Well, no one shoved us off and we hit the coal barge just the same. And say! There were splinters flying and glass cracking for a little while. Some of the boys were pretty badly scared. On invoicing the damage we found we had three window panes broken, several pieces of the siding torn loose and splintered up.

The current still stuck close to the shore for some distance after passing the barge, then it bore us out towards the middle of the stream and by the time we hit the Mississippi we were in mid-stream with a good current.

We floated along fine now and had no trouble until about sundown. We thought we would tie up for the night, so I loosened the ropes from the skiff and one of the boys loosened them from the cabin-boat, threw one rope down on the front porch and I took the other end and tied it to the skiff while Jim Wood stood on the front porch and held the other end and I started for the shore.

Well, the boat swung around out in the current and the first thing we knew the front end was hind end.

We were all getting a little bit excited, but I untied my end from the skiff and Jim hauled in the rope. I rowed around the front end again and Jim and John threw me the rope and we did the same thing over, the boat and all of us. There was more excitement by this time. Captain, steward, mate and al the deck hands were running around deck with ropes and giving orders. Hays and George Wood got stuck in one of the doors, both with a coil of rope in their hands, and both wanted to get through that door at the same time.

I do not know how many attempts we made to land, but it was "a plenty."

On looking ahead we saw a light on the bank and we began to yell, "Come out and land us; we can't land," and about that time we got opposite the light and a man came out in a skiff. We told him we had been trying to land for over two hours and couldn't.

He says, "Get on the back end of your boat and one of you hold the rope and throw me the other end."

2 C. B. P.

We did so and he tied the rope to the seat of his skiff and started to shore and that big old cabin-boat seemed to follow him just like a dog, without the least bit of trouble. It is a good deal in knowing how, eh?

He landed us near his cabin-boat. We found out that he and his pard, like us, were bound down the river.

This was our first landing and was near Wickliffe, Kentucky. So pleased were all of us to get to land and get tied up for the night that we all chipped in and gave him a dollar; besides, we brought out our jug with the snake medicine in and told him to help himself, which he did, and we called his pard and told him to do likewise. We found that this snake medicine, along the river, would do more than money at times. The man, Jack, and pard stayed and talked for a long while, and we found them both fine fellows and Jack said he would make us a pair of sweeps in the morning, and we gave him and pard another drink. We had supper and went to bed.

The next morning Jack went up the bank in the timber and cut two poles about fourteen feet long and brought them down and shaved the handles on the big ends and on the small ends attached a heavy piece of sheet iron which he found up along the railroad track somewhere. He then bored a ¾-inch hole in the gunnels out on the hind porch on each side about three feet from cabin so we would have room to stand between the cabin and the sweeps; then bored a ¾-inch hole about four feet from the handles on the sweeps and put a ¾-inch iron pin in gunnels and drove it down, letting it stick up so when the sweep was in place it extended out about two inches on top of the sweep. Now all we had to do was to take the sweep to one of these pins on each side and let the pin drop through the hole in each sweep and we were ready to go.

So tickled were we that we made up a jack-pot and gave him $2.00 and some more of the snake medicine. Before we started, to show his kindness towards us, he came marching into our boat with two pies and a roast duck. We all pulled out down the river together and for several days after floated along together and where one tied up the other tied up.

Say, do you know, we all wanted to work at those sweeps at once, and when it wasn't necessary; we had to call each other away from them. Why, we could take that old boat anywhere with those sweeps; could almost go straight across the river. We never had any more trouble about landing.

Our second landing was on the Missouri side of the river near Goose Bar, where James Wood brought to the boat a string of skip jack which he bought of a boy for brook trout. He showed them to me and I threw them in the river and for a minute Jim was pretty mad, but when I told him what they were and that they were no good to eat, he soon cooled off. We shoved off from here and floated down.

Landing No. 3 was at the upper end of Island No. 2 in the river. We were all a little out of tune here; some wanted to go on down the river at once and some wanted to stop and go hunting. But we pulled out and dropped down the river a few miles and tied up at the lower end of Island No. 2 and all but one went out on the Missouri side in the timber to hunt turkeys.

We came to a big canebrake where the cane was from six to twenty feet high, and as we could not penetrate it except by following cow paths through it, we all got separated in that canebrake and got lost. I came out somewhere on the opposite side of the canebrake and went about half a mile. As I was tired I sat down on a log and lit my pipe. I noticed that there were a number of trees blazed denoting a section line or some man's boundary line, so I took out my compass and decided, as it was getting late, to return to our boat. I started and traveled for some time and before I knew it I was back to the identical spot, for there was the log I had sat on and there were the blazed trees, and there were the burnt matches lying on the ground which I had thrown away.

Well, reader, I did that three different times, coming back to that same log every time and taking out my compass would start off again. But, do you know, that compass did not seem to point the right way. I finally found a road and followed it till I came to a rail fence and I looked at my compass and found that by following the fence it would take me to the river, which it did. But on looking at the river banks I knew I was somewhere above the cabin-boat, so I followed along down the river bank till I came to our boat. All the boys had found the boat but John Wood, and he had not got in yet, but arrived after dark.

I did not carry turkeys, but killed a few quail. John Wood saw three turkeys, but did not get a shot at them. We killed seven ducks here.

Our next landing was in a tree top on the Missouri side of the river, and as the wind had been high all day, and the waves on the river were also high, and as this was the most sheltered spot we could find, we pulled in and tied up for the night. But it was not a very pleasant place to be with the limbs rubbing against the bottom of the boat all night. We did not know what minute she might spring a leak and we examined the hull before we went to bed and even got up in the night and examined it several times. We were all glad when day came, with a bright, clear day ahead.

We pulled out again down the river and on December 3rd came to Belmont, Missouri, on the west bank of the river, While just across on the east bank stood Columbus, Kentucky. We stopped at Belmont to mail some letters home and after mailing them we saw a building with frosted windows which we entered. We saw a long bar with a lot of glasses and bottles sitting in front of a large mirror. So we walked up to the bar and looked through a large round glass with a handle on one side and tried to look back through the long, misty past to when General Grant with his army of over 3000 soldiers charged on Belmont away back in November, 1861.

But we could see nothing of him or any havoc he had done, although I had read that he lost some 400 or 500 men and the Johnnies something like 600. And that was General Grant's first victory and caused more excitement, sorrow and woe to the South than any victory during the great Civil War up to that time.

But on coming out and looking across the river at Columbus on the opposite bank, I could see a long brick wall still standing through which were great holes torn by cannon balls, and near the wall was a pile of canister and grape some four feet high, most of which were of the six and eight-pound style, with a lot of smaller. Near this pile of cannon balls were two or three weather-beaten crippled cannons, sad reminders of the great conflict that raged between the North and South from 1861 till '65.

As we floated on down the river I tried to locate

the place where he and his soldiers had disembarked
on the Missouri side, but time had obliterated everything.

We floated on down and our next stop was at
High Bluff, just above Hickman, Kentucky, where
we tier up for the night. We had by this time become so accustomed to the river and our cabin-boat
that all we did was to pull it out in the current and
let her drift—it mattered not which end was in front
or whether she was sideways, just so we were moving
down the river, now and then to pass a steamer or to
keep from lodging on sand bars. Two of us would
go out and take a few pulls at the sweeps and let
her go.

At times we were in company with a regular fleet,
all going down. Some days there would be from six
to ten cabin-boats all floating in all kinds of crafts:
Show boats, trading boats, cabin-boats, skiffs, etc.
I met a man in a skiff and he had it all covered over
with oilcloth and had cut holes on each side to give
him room to row and in daytime he would fasten
these strips up and at night would sleep in the skiff
and fasten these strips down. He had a coffee-pot,
skillet and a small sheet-iron stove and would tie up
to the bank and cook his meals and all he had to do
was to roll up his bedding in one end of the skiff,
throw in his few cooking utensils and he was ready
to go. This was his fifth trip down the river. He
started from Red Wing. He said he had been going
north every year and in the fall working in the wheat
fields of the Dakotas, and then after threshing time
drift down the river to winter.

I saw whole families—man, wife and three children—in a common open skiff not over fourteen feet
long, going down, camping on the banks when night

overtook them, without tent or shelter and with little in the way of bedding or cooking utensils.

Our next landing was on a sand-bar at the lower end of Island No. 8, and our next at a logging camp above New Madrid Bend. Here we all went out hunting and left Jim Wood to guard the cabin-boat. And here we met our first river tramp. On my return to the cabin-boat I saw on the bank a great big tall husky guy, who wanted to get on the boat. Jim was sitting on the front porch with his pump gun in his lap and I heard him say: "You are plenty close enough! Stay out there! You are not going to come up here." And he didn't, but soon walked away. After I came he wanted something to eat, but he didn't get it.

Now along the river these tramps will steal anything; even while you are asleep in your cabin will steal up in the night and cut a skiff loose. Or if you don't leave some one to watch your boat while you are gone, they will break in and take anything they want. For that reason we always left some one on the boat to guard it.

Here Jim Wood and I took our decoys and put them out on the west bank of the river to shoot ducks as it was the best place so far we had seen for ducks. The other boys wanted to go on, which they did, leaving Jim and me behind. We killed a shell drake, two or three Mallards, four or five grey ducks and a few teal, then took up our decoys and followed on down the river. When we found the boat it was after night and the boys had the lights lit and they had tied up at a logging camp about six miles above New Madrid on the Missouri side of the river.

The next morning we pulled out again and stopped at New Madrid to get our mail, which we had sent there and to mail some letters home. Here tied up to the wharf was one of the many show boats that ply up and down the river. Here also the railroad has built a track down in the river so you can float a cabin-boat over a flat car, which is let down in the river with cables and they draw cabin-boat and car and all up on the main track and take you across to the San Francis River, but we were bound down the river and did not cut across for the San Francis as many did.

We dropped down from New Madrid and tied up on the west side of Island No. 10. Also Dr. Kemble, two sons and daughter, whom we met several days previous farther up the river. They had floated down the Missouri from somewhere up about Kansas City. We had lost our friend Jack and pard who had made our sweeps, somewhere up the river. We all went hunting on Island No. 10 except George Wood, whom we left to guard the boat. None of us saw anything but Jim Wood; he flushed a bunch of turkeys in some thick brush about dark, but did not get a shot, so we all returned to the cabin-boat and had supper, which George had prepared for us.

He had roasted five ducks, one for each of us, besides fried potatoes, warm biscuits, corn, tomatoes and a pot of strong coffee. And say! There was not much left of those five ducks. What an appetite a man has after roaming around over logs, through the brush and briers. We all ate like a lot of bears.

After supper we talked it over and as it was a bright moonlight night, we decided we would go out and see if we could not get one or more of those turkeys by moonlight. So we all went about nine o'clock except one to watch our boat. We found out on that island in the big timber that it was not near as light as it was down along the river. And as turkeys generally roost in the tallest trees they can find, we struck for the tall trees. We scattered out and every now and then, bang! some one would shoot. Well, we shot at every knot on a limb and everything but a turkey. I did see one turkey fly out of a tree. I shot up at a big lump on a limb, but the turkey flew from the other side of the tree. One of the other boys scared a turkey out of a tree about the same way. We returned to the boat without any turkeys, but before going to bed we decided to get up early the next morning and scatter around through the timber and sit down; that the turkeys would be calling each other and we hoped by that way we would be able to connect with a turkey.

So just as it was breaking day the next morning all but one of us went forth after a turkey. Watts and I went together and the other boys scattered around through the woods. Watts was about two or three hundred yards northeast of where I was sitting on a log. We had been out there for probably two or three hours and not a turkey sound did I hear, although I never left the log or scarcely moved. All at once away at the upper end of the island I heard the bay of a hound, then more hounds, and I soon found out by the music they were making they were running my way. Now, thinks I, a deer. So I still sat there and all the time the hounds were drawing nearer. And maybe that wasn't music to me, on that still, clear morning.

I was just thinking what I would do to a deer if I got a chance when I was awakened from my reverie by the snap of a twig in front of me and on looking, not over thirty yards from where I sat, up run a red fox on a log. I made a move and at that the fox stopped and looked towards me. About that time there was the report of a gun and that fox fell off the log. I went up and picked him up and yelled over to Watts to come over that I'd killed a bear. He came over and I told him that I would have to "git" and to help put that fox in my hunting coat before the party who owned the hounds got there. So after cutting the pockets some we got the fox in and I struck for the cabin boat and told Watts to stay there till they came up and talk to them till I got to the boat with the fox.

The dogs, as soon as they came to where I shot the fox, lost the trail, of course, and were running around in a circle when the three men that the dogs belonged to rode up and said to Watts, "Did you shoot our fox?" He said no, but he heard a gun about 400 yards south of him. They talked awhile to him and rode around and around looking for it. One of them even came up to where our boat was tied, inquiring if any of us had seen anybody with a fox. By that time I had the fox skinned and his hid tacked up in the back room of our cabin-boat and the carcass was then floating down the river. He said that was the second fox within a week that had been shot in front of his dogs, and he wouldn't care so much for the fox, but he would like to have its brush to hang on the side of his bridle. About that time his horse, which he had left standing a short distance from our boat with his bridle rein over his head on the ground, started off on the run and he after it, and that was the last we saw of him or the hounds.

December 10th found us tied up to the bank at a logging camp about two miles above Mt. Pleasant, where we stayed two nights. Jim Wood killed a goose in a wheat field while George Wood, while watching the cabin-boat, saw a flock of geese coming up the river, grabbed his rifle and shot one, which fell in the river and drifted down about a mile before he could get a skiff and recover it, and as the current was quite swift here he had some hard rowing to do before he got back.

Somewhere up the river we had a tramp dog to come to our boat while we were tied to the bank. He was a big black and white dog, partly bull, for he showed it in his head and legs. And talk about your squirrel dogs! Well, he beat anything I had ever seen, and I had seen a few. He could see a squirrel farther through the timber and get one up a tree quicker than anything I had ever seen, and when he barked up Mr. Squirrel was always there and he never barked up the wrong tree, either. I have watched him watch squirrels jump from tree to tree, sometimes six or eight trees, but he always followed him and barked up at the tree the squirrel was on.

Well, he must have followed us for about a week, or as long as we tied to the east bank. On tying up it was not long until he was on hand and as quick as he saw our guns he would jump and bark and run around, as much as to say "I am ready." But by and by we lost him, as we did many other things along the river.

We pulled away from here and when we tied up again were about four miles below Mt. Pleasant on the Tennessee side of the river. Here was the best point on the river, so far, for geese. Here John Wood killed a number of ducks.

Thursday, December 13th, we passed upper Reelfoot landing and stopped on the Tennessee side of the river just below Gayoso, Missouri. Here Hays and Jim Wood killed a goose each and John Wood rowed across the river and hired a horse and went out in the sunken lands west to search for a hunting ground. On his return he reported seeing one deer and many deer and turkey signs, and said there were squirrels by the thousand. So on Saturday, December 15th, we loaded a tent, cooking utensils and grub into skiffs and rowed across the river, hired a team and wagon and went west of Gayoso towards the San Francis River about six miles, taking along with us, Dr. Kimble and one of his sons; the other son we left to guard our two cabin-boats.

We had floated down the river for several days previous to this, and December 17th found us in camp at a place they call Bull Island. We stayed there until Wednesday morning and having seen only one deer and some bear signs, we decided to get a team and move over to a hunter's cabin near a new railroad they were building from somewhere over on the San Francis River to Gayoso and Cottonwood Point. They called the place the "Blows," near which was Hurricane Ridge and Ingrams Ridge.

We pitched our tent near a little stagnant pool of water and a little way off was a hunter's cabin inhabited by a lone hunter who had a bunk of boards nailed to the wall in which he had gathered a lot of dry leaves and with only one blanket he was camping there. He had only a skillet and a coffee pot. There was no door to this log shack and you could see between the cracks in the logs. He had an old double barrel hammer shotgun with the extractor broken, and he carried a piece of iron in his pocket to knock out the brass shells which he used. He also had an old rifle about six feet long with the hammer gone.

How some people can go out in a lonely place like that with such an outfit and enjoy themselves, has always been a mystery to me, but he seemed to be right at home and seemingly just as happy as living in a brown-stone front.

The hermit, as I will call him, told us he would take us where there were plenty of deer within an hour. He had no ammunition so I gave him a shot sack full of powder and the boys gave him a lot of shot and he loaded up the few old brass shells he had and we were ready to start. We struck north of camp, leaving the Doctor to watch camp. When we got to the railroad we formed in line, keeping from 100 to 150 yards apart, and marched straight north. By so doing we thought if any of us should jump a deer some of us would be liable to get a shot at it.

We hadn't gone over a mile, all strung out—the hermit was on my left nearest to me, Watts was next to him on the left and John Wood was next, and George Wood next or the outer man on our left wing, while to my right Dr. Kimble's son was next to me and Jim Wood was the farthest man on my right. In this way we covered considerable ground. Well, as I said, we got about a mile the other side of the railroad and were walking through some pretty fair sized timber and it was reasonably clear of underbrush, when on looking ahead I saw ten deer, for I counted them.

An old doe was leading with two fawns following; behind her followed yearlings and two-year-olds. They were strung out in single file, walking along slowly, not having seen us. Yet when I pulled up my .44 rifle and commenced to shoot, at the first shot the deer broke and two two-year-olds came right towards me, and I was still shooting as they advanced. When near they swerved to the right and went so near to Dr. Kimble's son and Jim that I had to quit shooting.

About that time Dr. Kimble's son and Jim turned loose with their shot guns. Dr. Kimble's son had a double barrel shotgun and Jim a pump. The deer by this time were not over 20 or 30 yards from them. Well, Dr. Kimble's son shot both loads and Jim shot one load and downed one and instead of shooting at the other he fired another shot into the one after it had fallen. When I asked Jim why he didn't shoot at the other one he said he didn't think of it till it was gone. Dr. Kimble's son, in talking about it afterwards said, "I never expect to get another as good shot at a deer as that." And I don't think he will.

All the time I was shooting at the deer, turkeys were flying up all around me; there must have been quite a flock of them, for every now and then away one went, but we paid no attention to them, as we all had the buck fever and had it bad.

Well, we took the entrails out of the deer, tied its legs together, got a pole and run it through between its legs; Jim put one end of the pole on his shoulder and I the other end on my shoulder and started to camp. We had been there some time when here came Watts and John Wood with a big doe. Watts said that when I commenced shooting he saw the old doe and her two fawns coming straight at him and he said he didn't shoot until she was about a hundred feet from him, and that he downed her with the first shot, but for fear she would get away, he gave her another load. He said the two fawns still stood there looking at him and he was trying his best to find the shells in his hunting coat pocket, but search as he might he couldn't find them. All at once the fawns gave a little snort and hit their feet on the ground and they were gone. Then he said he found the shells.

That night we had venison for supper—yes, fried

venison, and we ate a whole hind quarter of the deer Jim had killed, at one meal. Dr. Kimble, who was cooking, was wondering if we would eat both deer all up so he wouldn't get any. He declared we would all be sick; but who ever got sick eating venison?

The next day we all went out in the same direction, but saw nothing in the deer line until we had started back to camp, when I heard a hound bay, a little to the north of us, and soon saw a deer coming towards us. The hermit, Jim and I were together, and as the deer got nearer I saw it had one front leg broken. We started to head it off as it turned on seeing us and about that time here came a hound with a long brass chain tied to her. Close behind the hound came three men on horseback on a dead run. As the deer swerved from us the front man on horseback fired and the deer ran a little piece to where a big tree had blown over and left quite a hole which was filled with water, and into this the deer fell. She was no more than down till the hound had her by the throat.

Some of the readers may want to know what those men had that big chain on the dog for: Well, if the chain hadn't been on, do you suppose they could keep up? Deer and dog would soon be out of sight. By having the chain on the dog they could keep in sight of the dog and of course the dog would keep on the track of the deer.

The next day John Wood and I went west over in the hurricane. Here, a few years before, a storm passed through, leveling the trees for about a quarter of a mile wide and I do not know how long. Anyway we could walk from tree to tree without getting on the ground. We supposed it would be a good place for deer and it was, but as there were so many tree-tops and the underbrush had grown up, it was almost impossible to get a shot. So we started back to camp.

We were walking along when all at once I heard John's rifle crack and just as I looked up I saw a deer go end over end several times like I had seen rabbits do when shot while running fast. On going up we found he had hit it in the neck and its neck was broken. It had jumped out of a tree-top and I was not looking that way when it started. We carried it to camp. The other boys came in soon; some had a turkey, others had nothing but squirrels.

Talk about squirrels! That was the greatest place I ever saw before or since for squirrels, both fox and grey, but the greys were the most plentiful. It was no uncommon thing to see five or six up one tree and the ground seemed to be covered with them. They would sit on a little low limb and you could almost reach them before they would offer to get out of your way. Or, sit on a log and bark at you, so close that you could hit them with a club. How many we killed I know not, but we did not kill as many as the reader would suppose, for what did we want with them when we had plenty of deer, turkey, geese and ducks?

We stayed in camp here till Sunday, December 23rd, when we returned to our cabin-boats on the river. But the night before we left camp our hermit neighbor stole a hind quarter of one of the deer and hid it somewhere out in the woods.

On Monday morning we cut loose and started for Cottonwood Point, but we tied up about one and a half miles below Linwood Landing, Tennessee, over night, and started down to Cottonwood Point next morning, tied up on the Missouri side of the river above the island, ate breakfast in Tennessee and supper in Missouri on Christmas day. Then pulled out for the lower end of the island. It was snowing hard.

December 27th we lay at the lower end of the island, just above Cottonwood Point. Next day we hired a negro who took Jim, John, Hays and I about five miles to the west out in the timber and swamps. We passed a sawmill and went on about three-quarters of a mile and stopped at a negro's cabin in the woods where the negro with the team was to stay till we came back. So we all struck out. Jim and I took a road that led off southwest through the woods and John and Hays struck out through the woods in another direction.

The snow was about six inches deep and one of those wet snows that clung to everything. The trees were so heavily loaded that in places the branches were bent almost to the ground. Every little shrub was loaded with snow and every now and then you would get a lot of it on your neck and it would melt and run down your back; so it wasn't very pleasant hunting under the circumstances.

Jim and I had not gone very far till we came to where we saw in the snow where an otter had crossed the road from one small lake to another and a flock of Mallards about that time flew over just above the tree-tops. We went on a little farther to a small lake and were walking along and we both saw a mink about the same time. He would make a jump and be in sight then he would be under the snow. We both started for him, I taking a shot now and then with my .44 as he would come in sight above the snow. We struck his trail and every few feet, when he made a jump, there would be a hole in the snow, then he would run under the snow a piece and then there would be another hole. But after awhile Jim got close enough to kill him with his pump gun.

We went back to the negro cabin and Watts was there, but John Wood had not showed up yet. So after waiting for some time, Jim and Hays decided they would walk back. So they left and I stayed at the negro hut till John came back, which he did in about an hour, and we started back to the river in the wagon.

We hadn't gone over two miles when on looking to one side over a fallen tree-top I saw seven turkeys standing, so I said to John, "See those turkeys?" and we let the negro drive on and John and I got out of the hind end of the wagon, and walked a few steps. We were both to draw on them, I was to count three and we were both to shoot. We both had rifles. Well, John shot, but my gun snapped, as I had no shell in the chamber; I had taken it out on entering the negro cabin when I had put my gun on the bed. Well, the turkeys flew away off south. John picked up the turkey he had killed and threw it in the wagon and told the negro to drive on home, and we struck out south after the turkeys.

We went half a mile or more before we struck their track, John taking one track while I took another. I tracked mine through the snow and every now and then I would get a glimpse of him away ahead up on a fallen tree and away he would go again. I never could get close enough to get a shot. After following about two miles I returned to the road and soon John returned. He had about the same experience after his turkey, so we walked to the river, got our turkey John had killed and went down to our boat.

Somewhere up the river we run into a whirlpool,

our cabin-boat was drawn in and went around and around like a top. Two of us went out and pulled at the sweeps, but still we went 'round and 'round. We were in it for some little time before we could get out, but finally by pulling hard on the sweeps we got out and shot on down the river.

The planters down in Kentucky and Tennessee let their land out to negroes to raise cotton on the shares. The negroes live in rude, rough log cabins, generally of one room, sometimes two rooms, with rough board floors, sometimes no floor at all except the ground, with one small window, sometimes two. They farm one mule or two mules. One mule is about five acres in cotton, while two mule is ten acres. The women and all the negro kids that are big enough, work in the cotton fields. And there are generally plenty of negro kids around a negro cabin. Some plantations have a cabin every five or ten acres, while other planters have their negro quarters near their own.

The planter furnishes everything. The negroes are furnished corn meal, great slabs of salt pork, four to six inches through, beans, coffee, and sugar now and then. After the cotton is all picked the planter settles up with them and those negroes think they are lucky if their master, as they call the planter, gives them ten or fifteen dollars in cash. The planters seem to be pretty good in figures.

We lay at Cottonwood Point for several days and on December 28th we hailed the Ora Lee and she shoved out her gangplank, a lot of negroes ran out and grabbed our trunks—that is, Jim Wood's, Hays' and mine—and carried them aboard. The bell gave a few jingles and the snout of the Ora Lee swung out in the channel and we were soon on our way toward home, leaving George and John Wood still aboard the Industry. The fare from Cottonwood Point to Cairo was $3.50.

On the way up the river we met great ice floes. In places they extended almost from shore to shore, and at night the Ora Lee kept her searchlight busy throwing it here then there, trying to dodge the ice as much as possible. Every now and then we could feel the shock and could hear the ice breaking and grinding against her as she plowed her way through the great fields of ice.

We arrived at Cairo about ten o'clock Sunday night, where we bought tickets for home and left Cairo at 12:37 a. m.

On the San Francis River.

John and George Wood, after we left for home, floated on down to the mouth of the San Francis River and as the Mississippi River was higher than the San Francis, they floated up the San Francis about six miles, where they stayed a week or so. They sold the cabin-boat to a man for $25, and had to wait till he had chopped enough cord wood to pay for it.

If any one has the time and inclination and likes outdoor life, he will find no trip that he can make that will be enjoyed better than a trip down the Mississippi in a cabin-boat. Of course the game laws now are different. At that time you did not need a hunting license; you could hunt where you pleased. You could sell your game if you wished and you were never molested. I have been hunting since down in that country a number of times and the last time I was down I had to take out a $25 non-resident hunting license and to get one I had to give a $200 bond signed by two residents as security that I would not break any of the game or fish laws of the state.

CHAPTER II.

A Trip Down the Yukon.

CIRCLE CITY, a few years ago, was the largest "Log Cabin Town" in the world. It is the supply point for the extensive Placer Mines, fifty miles west near the head of Deadwood, Mastodon, Henderson, Eagle and Mammoth Creeks.

To pack an outfit to these mines and double trip it was no small task, requiring eight days. The trail follows across long stretches of moss covered tundra, where nearly every step in the mud found bottom on ice or frozen ground.

Along the summit of narrow ridges, across deep, swift, ice-cold creeks through jungles of willow, level flats of birch and aspen, with gloves on the hands and a mosquito net over the face, the trip is one to try the patience and test the endurance of any "Old Timer."

But once in the headquarters, the struggle is soon forgotten in the pleasure and the excitement of the chase over the hills after caribou; and more, the thrill when the game is sighted at midnight.

When done here with the camera and rifle, returning to Circle, we launch the boat and away we go floating on the broad bosom of the "Great Yukon" wending its way to the Bering Sea, 1,500 miles from Circle.

Two days will float us to Fort Yukon, ninety miles. Here the Porcupine River enters the Yukon and I have been told that this place lies six miles within the Arctic Circle. Here the Yukon sweeps to the south, sweeping across wide flats, butting against high, ragged cliffs and low grass covered hills.

Islands are plentiful and it puzzles an expert in Yukon navigation to keep in the right channel.

Ducks, geese, swan, and seagulls are plentiful; but, let us pull into camp at the mouth of a small slough, cast a small hook, and Oh, Ho, a fine grayling. Next cast a heavy trolling spoon, swing it slowly— look out there, keep your line steady, let him play a little, gently bring him ashore; there now—a 15-pound pickerel.

Yes, fish three times a day if we want them.

For a change, go into the timber, get a few pine squirrels and a blue grouse, then switch to ducks and geese and look out for eggs. This section is known as the "Yukon Flats," and ducks, geese and swan breed here. Seagulls also nest on the gravel bars.

Seventy-five miles and we arrive at Nuk-lak-a-yet, a trading post. From here we leave the North Channel and at last camp at the mouth of a slough to prospect and fish a little. We are here four days, during which time my partner and I took several strolls across the country. Not a human being did we see. We were alone with nature. I discovered a lake, two miles in length and one mile in width, fringed with willows and heavy timber. This lake was alive with trout and the muskrats could be seen everywhere.

Oh, what a time, during the four days, I caught 600 pounds of pickerel—130 fish. Talk about fun, yes, and lost two trolls, made three more of wire nails and lost them too. This was in October and the fish would freeze at night.

We pulled out for Rampart and took five days to float down the river. Slush ice was gathering, the cold was pinching and we soon had our boats hauled up. We were held up for the winter and our fish— well I guess not, sold out for $150.00 and had fresh fish all winter.

Yes, the cold, quiet winter is over. The miners have rehearsed their yarns and smoked the pipe of peace. They hitch their dog teams to the sleigh and pull out for the mines, eight miles away, and in a few days I follow with my big 8 x 10 camera.

The deep mines have been worked during the winter and now the dumps are being shoveled into the sluice boxes, which are cleaned at night and what a sight to see the yellow stuff, some of the nuggets weighing fifty pounds.

Views of the mines are secured and your Uncle Doc floats away alone; the river is high and swift, great banks of ice line the shore in places thirty feet high; the river banks have been torn, trees uprooted and splintered, and every spring sees old islands torn away, new ones formed, channels turned, cakes of 100 feet square and 6 feet thick lodged upon gravel bars. This, and much more, is the scene witnessed every spring when the icy fetters are loosened in the mighty river and start, with a force no human power can resist, with crash and jam it rushes on its way to the sea.

Rampart is a large mining camp, located near the mouth of Big Minook Creek and four hundred miles below Circle.

I make the remainder of my trip alone. I will give some dates and distances from one place to another, and the reader can see that I was in no particular hurry to end this most delightful trip, which, to the timid, might seem a dangerous and hazardous one. But, it was simply my own manner of spending my summer vacation.

Leaving Rampart May 23d, I reached Tanana River the 29th. This river, and some of its tributaries, are the scene of active mining operations. Fort Gibbons is located on the opposite side of the Yukon (North). We glide along camping in time to have trout or grayling for supper.

The 31st of May we passed Del-sin-e-wat River. On the first of June we passed the Mel-o-zee and next day halt at the Indian Village called "Noo-hal-ta-til-ton." Here I turned my camera upon some curious old Indian graves.

The better class of Indians throughout this Arctic region place the body in a box, then build a small house into which is placed the box with some of the belongings. Others place the box on a low platform with a roof over it, and others place the box on the ground. At one place a pen had been made of split slabs, the body placed in this enclosed in a box and the pen filled with dirt, while near by a muzzle loading double barrel shot gun was tied to the top of a post and a roof over it. In some places could be seen all kinds of childish trinkets, jingle bells, strings of beads, small spears, plows and arrows and snow shoes. Dishes, kettles, knives, forks and spoons were common.

June 4th. Pass Koyakuk River, also Pickett Station, one of the many places where the steamers get wood.

June 5th. Arrive at Nulatta, an Indian Village, trading post and mission. Here I outwitted the natives. The village is located at the base of a high bluff, upon which is the cemetery. The natives fled at sight of my camera and as I wanted a photo of the decorated graves I set out at daylight, ascending the high cut bank and trained my camera on what I wanted and at the first streak of sunshine I pressed the bulb. The thing was done and I was back to camp in the village before it was awake. Had I been caught I don't know that my life would have been worth 30 cents. Poor benighted souls, many of them firmly believe that to have a photo taken means death within a year.

June 14th. Arrive at Anvic, a village and mission at the mouth of Anvic River, 150 miles below Nulatto. On the way from Nulatto, we pass Kol-tag, a small station and coal mine fifty miles above Anvic and Grayling a wood station where the natives cut wood and load it onto barges.

June 15th. Arrive at the Catholic Mission, forty miles below Anvic.

June 18th. Arrive at Pi-e-mute, a small village and vacant, as the whole population is out hunting and fishing. Here I entered the large underground room, the "Ka-zhin," which is used as main winter quarters. Here are two cemeteries, the original and the new. In the former is seen all the crude methods and paraphernalia of the savage and in the latter, quite a mark of civilizing influence. This village, I was told, is the boundary between the upper Malamost Indians and the lower river tribes.

June 21st. At Russian Mission, sixty-five miles, Holy Cross Mission (Catholic). Here is a large church of imposing proportions and appearance. I believe the village is called I-kog-a-mute. By permission of the priest, I photographed both the church and the village.

June 22nd, 11 p. m. Just got my camp set when I heard an awful racket just across the slough from camp. I seized my 30-40 and ran out and found the noise was caused by a huge cinnamon bear and the way he knocked the chunks about in trying to bid me a hasty goodnight was a caution. At a distance of 150 paces I fired two shots at him but failed to puncture his ugly carcass as far as I know.

We are now below the best game section, the country is more smooth, mountain ranges are few and short but bears are quite plentiful. From here to Bering Sea the current is not so swift and the scenery is more of a kind and color.

Hudson Bay Co. York Boat.

June 23d. Halt in a slough and take a stroll over what looked like a dry expanse of barren tundra, but not so dry after all, as the water slushed under my rubber boots. But what desolation and solitude. The level barren ground was covered only with a scant growth of hard, colorless moss, in the near distance were barren hills and ridges. I looked for some form of life and beauty, but I only found two or three small black butterflies and a few yellow flowers. I became disgusted and returned to my boat.

June 25th. Halt at Andrewsky, a village at the mouth of the river of that name. One-half mile above the mouth are large ware houses in which goods are stored for the winter. From here steamers leave as soon as the Yukon is open for up river points and before the ice leaves Bering Sea.

June 30th. Seventy-five miles below Andrewsky. Slow, sure enough, but some rain with the wind blowing up stream ran me into camp every time.

July 1st. Enter Aphoon slough. This is the most northern channel, the right hand arm of the Yukon and from here we have very slow current and to move along, we must often lean to the oars.

At 2 o'clock p. m. we arrive at Hamilton, where a native tells us that it is twenty-five miles to the sea.

July 2nd, 2 p. m. At Koat-lik. At the mouth of that river this place contains about fifty people of Eskimos and a general mix up of Indian and Russian blood, dressed in all styles, from calico to sealskin and I took a photo of several. This place was founded more than a hundred years ago by the Russian traders and it certainly looks that age.

Four miles from Koat-lik and I pull my good old canvas boat out into the salty waters of Bering Sea.

Good-bye, Mighty Yukon. I have been borne along upon your placid bosom nearly 2,500 miles, but now you have cast me upon the bosom of your "Alma-Mater," the restless, ever restless, surging ocean.

The banks are only a few feet high and back

for many miles extends a level almost barren tundra of stunted moss. The shore in many places is strewn and piled high with all manner of drift and wreckage, and every now and then can be seen dead seals which have been wounded by native hunters, who, when they find a carcass skin, cut it up for food.

July 9th. Pass Point Romanoff, only sixty miles from Koat-lik. Some rain and choppy sea has kept me in camp.

July 10th. Enter the "Canal" and pitch my tent. Here I leave the open sea. The canal is the channel forming St. Michael Island, upon which St. Michael is located twenty-seven miles away. At high tide steamers pass through and thus save the risk of twenty-five miles at sea.

10 P. M. The tide has turned and I pull out as this tide will carry me to the bay near St. Michael. The ever present mosquito bothers me some, but on I go, and at this, 6 a. m., July 5th, I pitched my tent at St. Michaels.

St. Michaels is quite a trading and distributing point. It is also military headquarters for Alaska. At the time of this trip three large trading companies were represented by lines of steamers and with large ware houses and hotels.

Many Russians, Americans and natives reside here, the natives coming from hundreds of miles away on the coast to trade. Here can be seen furs of all kinds, from the marten to the polar bear; also whalebone, walrus tusk and all kinds of trinkets carved in ivory.

Looking around I find many campers, old timers and prospectors and all seem to be enjoying themselves, as only those who battle with the rough side of life can understand.

Aug. 20th. Aboard a schooner bound for Cape Nome. I am soon sea-sick and crawl into my bunk and the ring of the supper bell failed to drag me out.

Aug. 22nd, 5 a. m. Here I am at Nome City, stretching along the shore a motly maze of tents and houses, a distance of five miles, Snake River coming into the sea near the western suburbs and Nome River near the eastern where the military barracks are being built.

In a short time after I come ashore I regaled myself on a 50-cent lunch, shouldered my camera and struck out. Nome, at this time, is a quagmire, located upon the level tundra and the streets are almost impassable, no sidewalks. I jump from a board to a box and from there to a stump but I get there just the same. I go across Nome River over a bridge, visit the barracks, thence back and follow a slushy railroad to Anvil City, five miles northwest, and return.

Aug. 23d. On board a steam schooner bound for St. Michaels. From on deck can be seen plainly the mining machinery for a distance of three miles sluicing the beach sands and gravel for gold.

Aug. 24th, 8 a. m. At "Chinic" and anchor in Gollivan Bay. At the head of this bay, twenty miles, is a large mining camp.

Aug. 25th, 5 a. m. At St. Michaels and now I can kill time for a month.

Sept. 22nd. All aboard the steamship, Robert-Dollar.

Sept. 28th. Back to Nome, aboard four days before steaming out.

Oct. 14th, midnight. Steam out, and all this time I have been penned up with three hundred others waiting to get away, and a dreary old time we have had.

Oct. 17th. At Dutch Harbor, 800 miles from St. Michaels, in the Alieutian Islands. This place is headquarters for the fur company leasing the seal islands. Whaling vessels also call here for supplies. I get busy with my camera and visit Ounalaska, three miles away. This is an old trading post and here, as at many other Alaskan towns, the old muzzle loading cannon are lying around like so many old logs.

Oct. 20th. Steam out and now for a long stretch at sea.

Oct. 28th, 11 p. m. At Port Townsend, Washington.

Oct. 29th, 6 p. m. In Seattle.

Nov. 1st. All aboard for Juneau, nine hundred miles.

Nov. 5th. At Juneau and I am home once again, and now, indulgent readers, how does the trip described appeal to you as to your idea of a good time?

This trip totals a distance of 6,500 miles across the wild waters and on the sea, and this is only one of three of the same kind, but if you want to follow in your Uncle's past footsteps, they will lead you across barren waters, down into the deep recesses of rock bound canyons and to the dizzy heights of 13,000 feet upon the mountain tops, capped with eternal snow.

CHAPTER III.

The Cabin Boat.

THERE are many kinds of house and cabin boats. Of the 15,000 odd floating homes on the Mississippi and its tributaries, not many are alike. Each builder has his own notions —or lack of them—and the result is a great diversity of models. Before describing one of these in detail, brief mention may be made of the commonest shapes, sizes and uses.

Storeboats and showboats are the largest cabin boats on the Mississippi and Ohio Rivers. Several of them are 100 or even 200 feet long, from 18 to 50 feet wide, and draw up to five feet of water at the load line. Boats of this size are floated down stream with the current, guided by great oars—sweeps—and swung in and out of landing by long ropes, anchor lines and adroit use of currents. A considerable proportion of the river people, however, have gasoline or steamboat tenders for their cabinboats, which reduce the difficulties of navigation of even small boats very materially. In recent years, power house-boats have appeared in numbers.

From the huge showboats' size, the cabin boats range down to mere skiffs or scows ten or twelve feet long and covered with "rag-cabins" or "paper-shacks" —canvas and tar paper shelters. Probably 90 per cent of the Mississippi basin cabinboats are less than forty feet long, and more than eighteen feet long. Two hundred years of house boating has taught the "shanty-boater" that the best size for river house-boats lies somewhere between these figures. The larger the boat the more difficult it is to "man-handle."

Building a Cabin on a Scow.

4 C. B. P.

The largest cabin boats—the showboats—are simply huge scows, decked and cabined. Here and there one discovers a "model hull" with a round bottom, and shaped something like a small canal boat. The commonest type of medium sized cabinboat is the scow hull and box cabin. There are some converted steamboats and gasoline boats. A few "double-hulls" have been built—a "double hull" is a catamaran, or a platform on which a cabin is erected, built on two long narrow hulls. Some of the most comfortable and safest, "one man" boats, are large skiffs, covered from the stern by low cabins over three-fourths of their length and sometimes decked the rest of the way.

One must decide first of all about what type of boat he wants or needs for his purpose. If it is a journey for pleasure, the boat to serve merely as a traveling camp, the number of persons going, their sex, and the amount of space required, must be figured out. A boat twenty feet long and seven feet wide will carry one man most comfortably; two could travel in it without impossible crowding. A boat twenty-four feet long, and eight feet wide, with a sixteen-foot cabin is ample for two. A boat twenty-eight feet long, nine feet wide and having a cabin nineteen feet long, divided into two rooms, has fair accommodations for four persons. I have seen a man living on a shantyboat twelve feet long, four feet wide and having a cabin eight feet long. Two painters and their wives left Dixon, Ill., in a boat sixteen feet long, seven feet wide and having a cabin eleven feet long. The four of them carried the boat around a mill dam on Rock River, where they started. A sheet of canvas served as a partition at night, being rolled up to the carlins of the roof by day. They traveled to far below Cairo in this. I have lived for weeks in

Cabin Boats in Little Eddy.

a skiff which I covered with a low canvass roof on hoops at night, or during bad weather.

If one needs more than mere living space, of course, allowance must be made for the extra size. A man "junking" the river can handle a boat thirty feet long, ten feet wide and loaded with tons of iron, brass, bones and bottles. Two men would not want a boat more than thirty-five feet long for a junking trip and a thirty-foot boat would serve. If one makes photographs for money along the way, a "studio" and dark room should be provided. The studio may be used between times as a dining room and kitchen, but it must be large enough to accommodate a large family during a sitting. A photograph boat is some-times sixty feet long, fifteen feet wide and has a cabin forty-five feet long, divided into gasoline en-gine room, living rooms, dark room and pantry (with passageway between) and studio. A storeboat must be large enough to carry the stock, and one room, at the bow, must have shelves, floor space, counters, and standing room. One boat, on the Mississippi River has a sales room sixty feet long, another a room only eight feet square.

For one's first trip it is better not to be over-ambitious. Of two boats that "will do," the smaller should be taken, other things being equal. A twenty-five foot boat will carry junk of surprising quantity, if properly stowed—many a boat of this size goes into New Orleans with more than $200 worth of brass, copper and other stuff for sale.

Necessarily, it is difficult to give exact advice as to the size of boat needed by a would-be tripper, but in any event, for those who have had no experience "tripping," a boat thirty-five feet long should be the limit in size, and even that length will sometimes prove embarassing in some winds and currents during the first weeks of the journey. A boat from twenty-five to thirty feet long and eight or ten feet wide would seem to be the best size for ordinary river tripping and river business.

There are three ways of getting a cabin boat—buying, building or having built. Each way has its advantages.

First, let us consider buying a boat.

A large percentage of cabinboats in the Mississippi basin are for sale. Excellent boats are always to be had at certain well known "shantyboat" towns, of which there are many on the rivers. Thus Pittsburg, Cincinnati, Evansville and Cairo on the Ohio; Burlington, St. Louis (Little Oklahoma), Memphis, Helena, Arkansas City, Vicksburg, Baton Rouge, Plaquemine, and New Orleans on the Mississippi; Kansas City on the Missouri; Decatur on the Tennessee, and other points are "shantyboat towns," from the riverman's viewpoint. Here, cabin boats may be found in greater or less number, usually some of them for sale.

The further down the river, the cheaper the boats, for their possible journey has been shortened. Thus the value of a boat starting at Pittsburg, may be $150; at Memphis its value may be only $75; at Baton Rouge $40; at New Orleans $10.

A boat may change hands a dozen times or more in its trip from Pittsburg, Pa., or Burlington, Ia., to New Orleans. The builder may be an "upper river" man, with no desire to go out of the Ohio or below St. Louis. He will sell out at Evansville, Paducah, Cairo or St. Louis, return to his starting point and build a new boat. He may be a "sport"—somebody traveling for fun. In that case he may go clear to Memphis or Helena before selling out. The second owner may work the boat down only a few miles, fishing or trapping for a year or two on fifty miles of river. A third owner may carry the boat no further than the second. A fourth may work between Arkansas City and Vicksburg only. After five years, perhaps, somebody buys it cheap, loads it with junk, trips it down to New Orleans and there it is broken up for fire wood or run up on the bank and used by a darkey as a home.

One must consider the condition of the boat with regard to the service for which it is intended. A poplar boat goes fast when it begins to rot. But a poplar boat a year old and well built, will last through a winter—which is all a mere tripper asks of his boat. If it sells for anything at the end of the journey, that is profit.

In buying a boat, consider as far as possible its previous history. The hull is of first importance. If it is sound and strong the boat is worth having, but if it is rotten, or if it leaks, then have a care about purchasing it. Of course if one plank is broken in a hull otherwise sound, that plank may be replaced; or if the leak is from cracks, the cracks can be caulked. A boat offered for $20 may be repaired for $20.

A shanty boater knows that $5.00 worth of paint will cover $100 worth of defects. A very pretty cabinboat which I saw at Memphis—bright, clean, shapely and attractive—was so rotten that a penknife blade went clear to the handle in the hull below the water line. It was sold for $50 on its looks; a dirty boat a few rods away was offered for $40—the latter one would weather a cyclone, and be as pretty, after scrubbing and painting. The intrinsic values were as 5 to 100.

A Model Hull Shanty Boat on Tennessee River.

If the hull is sound, a poor cabin can be forgiven. It would pay to put a new cabin on some hulls. The cabin one lives in on the river for a winter, should be tight and warm. It must be strong enough to stand the wrenching of gales that unroof barns and throw down trees.

Paint and a lining of red building paper will make the cabin wind-tight; tar or patent roofing or canvas will keep out the rain which falls on the cabin top. But if the cabin is properly built, this repairing will not be necessary. Not one in a hundred shanty-boats is "tight." Usually a purchaser must have the cabin seams and hulls cracks stopped up—caulked.

A partition through the middle of a cabin strengthens it very much. A few braces from the top of the gunwale inside the cabin to the frame uprights. window framing and corner posts, will add greatly to the strength of the cabin. If one buys with the idea that repairs, painting and changes must be made, a very good boat can usually be had at a reasonable price, when all is counted up.

At Rosedale, Miss., one of the men I tripped with, bought a sound unpainted boat, 15 feet long, 7 feet wide, for $15.00, and weathered bad storms in it. It was a trapper's boat, originally, and served for a one-man boat as well as one costing a hundred dollars, although the quarters were small.

CHAPTER IV.

How to Build a Cabin Boat.

IF one is fairly handy with tools—if he can draw straight lines with a square, saw to a line, plane to an edge and drive nails—he can build his own cabin-boat. It will be some cheaper to do this than to hire the boat built, and is likely to be as cheap as buying one. A new boat, well built, is a satisfaction and comfort in the presence of drift, ice or a cyclone.

The boat which seems best from the tripper's point of view is 28 feet 8 inches long, 9 feet wide, and 30 inches deep in the hold. The cabin is 18 feet 10 inches long, 8 feet 6 inches wide and 6 feet 5 inches between floor and carlins (rafters). The cabin should be divided into two rooms. A cabin of this length allows a deck at the bow with a length of 5 feet 4 inches and at the stern of 4 feet 4 inches.

To build a boat of this type the following lumber and material are needed, net measurements. In a subsequent chapter, a light hull will be described; the one here described is the usual heavy Mississippi river construction.

The Hull—Ironware, Etc.

Four right angle straps, $1\frac{1}{2}$-inch wide, $\frac{1}{2}$-inch thick, 2 feet long on each angle; twelve $5\frac{1}{2}$-inch $\frac{3}{8}$-inch bolts; ten pounds 5-inch nails for stringers; twenty pounds 7-inch nails for bottom plank; eight pounds 8-inch nails for scarfs; twenty 9-inch spikes for bumpers; twenty-four 20-inch $\frac{3}{8}$-inch iron spikes, or bolts, for strakes; twenty-four 28-inch ⅜-inch bolts; twenty pounds 2-inch nails for siding and roofing; ten pounds 3-inch nails for flooring; twenty-five pounds white lead; two and one-half gallons outside paint; two gallons paint for hull (outside); two gallons barn paint for inside hull; five quarts inside paint for cabin; 100 feet twisted cotton rope for caulking.

Lumber, for Hull.

Two timbers, 28' long, 3" thick, 9" wide (D).

Two timbers, 28' long, 3" thick upper side, 4" thick lower side, 12" wide and cut   (C).

Two timbers, 25' 6" long, 4" thick, 9" wide (B).

(In above figures, observe the measure is net, and that if scarfing, or "splicing," is necessary, overlap must be allowed.)

Two timbers, 9' long, 12" x 4" (E).

155' lineal measure, 6" x 2" scantling for stringers (F).   (Hemlock will do.)

Two-inch planking, planed both sides, to cut 9' 2" long.   The width does not matter so much. However, the narrower the plank, down to, say four inches, the less likelihood of checking.   The plank must cover the bottom and rakes, a surface of about 30 feet length (good measure) 9' 2" wide.

Four pieces of oak, 42" long by 4" x 4" (timberheads).

Two 5" x 5" x 32" long oak pieces (oar pin heads).

Five hemlock plank, 5" x 1½" by 9' (deck beams).

Flooring to cover 28' x 9' (decks and cabin floor).

Lumber for Cabin.

24 uprights—4' 4" long, 2" x 1½".

12 carlins (6" wide. center, 2" ends), 9' 2" long.

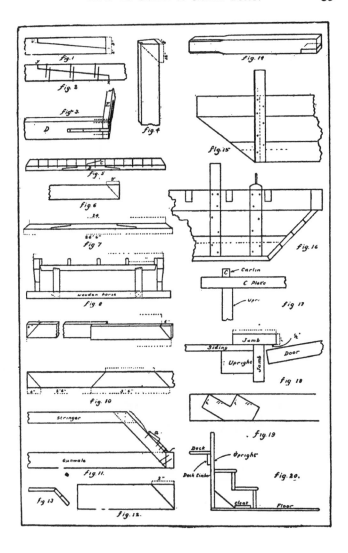

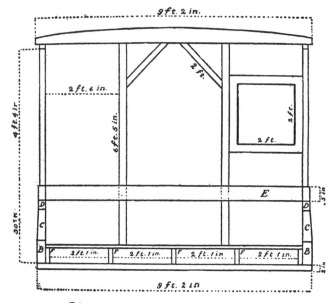

Diagram of end of Houseboat.

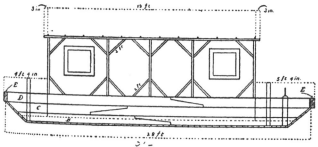

Diagram of side of Houseboat

50′ lineal measure board, 4″ wide, 1″ thick (mop board).

36 struts, 2′ long, sawed in 45 degree mitre box (2″ x 1″).

90′ lineal measure, 2″ x 1½″ spruce for plates.

Doors and windows to suit taste. (See chapter description.)

⅜″ matched siding (to cover 415 square feet; depends on width).

Building paper to lay on under siding may be put on, and some kind of roofing should be laid on the top.

If the cabin is partitioned off, other material will be needed, as uprights, siding, etc.

The hull is constructed first. The most convenient way is to build it upside down. The gunwale timbers (D), if in one piece, are laid edge down on three or four 10-foot long carpenter's horses, parallel and eight feet six inches apart.

If the timbers are not long enough they must be "scarfed" as indicated in diagram one (XXX). It may be necessary to have two scarfs in each of the side lines of timber. For each scarf an allowance of three feet extra length of plank must be made to make up for overlap. To make a scarf in the gunwale plank, "square up" one of the planks (D) by marking with a square and sawing off each end without waste. Then "square up" one end of the second piece. Then saw into the edge of one plank three feet from the end to a depth of exactly two inches. From the bottom of the slash to a point at the end two inches from the opposite edge, draw a straight line. (Fig. 1.)

Then saw the diagonal line. A similar cut is made in the next timber, so that the two ends will lap. (Fig. 2.)

If it is necessary to use three lengths of planking, two scarfs must be made, and six feet net extra length allowed for each gunwale. When the gunwales have been sawed to fit, smear the joints with white lead, lay three or four strands of frayed cotton rope from y to z (Fig. 2) and spike the scarfs with eight-inch spikes, as indicated in Fig. 2.

Now the bumpers must be fitted. The two bumper timbers (E) exactly nine feet long, are spiked on the ends of the gunwales. (Fig. 3.) When the bumpers are in place, put straps of iron around each corner to tie the bumper to the gunwale. The straps should be one and one-half inch wide, half an inch thick and at least two feet long on each side of the angle. They are bolted to the bumper and gunwale with five inch, quarter-inch bolts, three on each angle. These straps will prevent the bumpers from being jerked off.

The two side planks (C) (middle strakes) are cut to fit their place. The three-inch edge fits the three-inch edge of the gunwale. They must be sawed for the rake of the bow and stern. The end of one plank is "squared up" and then cut from the three-inch hedge to a point one foot from the end of the four-inch edge. (Fig. 4.)

These planks are scarfed till of the requisite length —28 feet on the 3-inch edge, and 26 feet on the 4-inch edge. The gunwale bottom edges are smeared with white lead and strands of frayed cotton rope laid along the lead. Then the side strakes are rested on the gunwales (Fig. 5). When the two rows of strakes are in place, they should be fastened with $\frac{3}{8}$-inch iron spikes, 20 inches long, driven into quarter-inch holes bored down through the sides at intervals of 2 feet (Fig. 5).

The plank for the bottom strakes (B) are then shaped. One end is "squared up," and then sawed diagonally from the end of one edge to the opposite edge 9 inches from the end (Fig. 6).

If necessary, the timber is scarfed to a length of 25 feet 6 inches on the long edge. Saw a diagonal as in Fig. 6, but from the opposite end. Fig. 7 represents the bottom plank.

When the planks have been sawed for scarfing and to fit, they are laid long edge down on the short edge of the plank C. There they are spiked fast with 28-inch long ⅜-inch bolts driven through quarter-inch holes bored through the planks at intervals of 2 feet.

In making scarfs, care should be taken to "break the joints" so that no two scarfs are on the same perpendicular, a scarf being necessarily weaker than solid timber, in boring holes for the bolts care should be taken not to strike scarfing spikes.

Stays (any boards long enough) are nailed to the sides to hold the outside edges of the sides exactly 9 feet 2 inches apart, while the stringers are put in, bumpers nailed and strapped on and planking nailed fast.

The bumpers (E) are spiked across the ends of the gunwales. The iron straps are bolted on the angles.

The stringers (F) are 6 inches wide. Four temporary "arches" should be nailed inside the hull with their tops just 6 inches below the level of the bottom. On these arches the stringers—F, F, F, F, F,—are laid, two against the hull sides, the others down the center in parallels 2 feet 1 inch apart from center to center of the stringers (Fig. 8).

The arches support the stringers while they are being fitted and fastened in place. One of the 13-foot

long hemlock planks is squared up without waste at
each end. Then 6 inches from one end make a mark
on one edge. From this mark draw a line diagonally
back to the end of the other edge. Saw off the triangular block, and lay the plank long edge down on
the arches next to the hull side. Square up one end
of another plank, and lay this end, end-to against the
plank in place, and the end of the second plank will
project beyond the end of the hull. Mark down the
side of the plank on the diagonal end of the bottom
strake of the hull, and saw on the line (Fig. 10).
Then nail to the bottom strake with the edge flush.

In the three inside rows of stringers, instead of
matching the planks end to end, lap them side to side,
leaving just length enough for diagonals at each end
—nail the laps with eight nails each.

Four pieces must now be prepared to stiffen the
bow and stern bottom planks. Square up the end of a
6-inch hemlock plank, draw a line diagonally from the
end at one end to a point 6 inches from the same end
on the opposite edge. Saw off the triangular block,
and measure 2 feet 6 inches along the plank from
the short edge. Mark it. Mark a place 6 inches
further along the edge; draw a line square across the
plank from the second mark, and then draw a line
diagonally back to the 2 feet 6 inches mark. Saw the
diagonal, and then repeat till the six pieces required
are in hand (Fig. 11). This gives six pieces 3 feet
6 inches on the long edge, and 2 feet 6 inches on the
short edge.

These pieces are laid beside the stringer ends with
their short sides parallel to the rake of the bow, one
diagonal end against a bumper, the other diagonal end
parallel to the bottom of the boat. (Fig. 12.) The
pieces are nailed or bolted to the stringers, and spiked
stoutly to the bumper as indicated in Fig. 12.

In the bottom of each center line of stringers three notches 3 inches wide, 1 inch deep are cut, one near the middle, one near each end of each stringer, so that water can flow freely across the bottom to the pump wells in case of a leak.

Now put on the planking. The plank adjoining the bumper must be fitted first. One edge is beveled with a draw knife and smoothed with a plane, the bevel extending two inches down the side of the plank (I on I) (Fig. 13).

This beveled edge lies against the bow bumper— either end of the hull will serve as bow at this stage. The beveled edge of the plank and the rake of the sides on which the plank is to rest are smeared with white lead, and a shredded strand of cotton rope, dipped in the lead, is laid along the bumper, along the rake of the sides and along the bottom edges. The plank is laid on the diagonal ends of the sides, with the bevel flat side to the bumper against the rope (Fig. I.). Set close and nail fast. The next plank is beveled from each side to a line drawn down the center of one edge, the bevel being one-sixteenth of an inch deep on the sides (a, Fig. 11).

Now bevel the edge of the next plank so that there will be a blunt edge. This is done by drawing a line down the center of the edge of a plank—one inch from either side—and then beveling from each side to the line. The bevel should not be more than an eighth of an inch on either side, and a sixteenth of an inch is enough—do it with a plane. The plank is then put on the hull with the under edge of the bevel resting on the upper edge of the plank already in place (See a, Fig. 11).

Nail fast as seen in the figure on strakes and

5 C. B. P.

stringers, white lead the bevel and then force the plank down into place, nailing fast, with a total of three 5-inch nails to each stringer and bottom strake—twenty-one nails in all. This is "jumping the plank", and it makes a water tight joint. If the strakes are carefully leaded and cotton strands used at the contacts, the hull cannot leak. All the planks are put on by "jumping" till the foot of the rake is reached, where another bevel must be made, against which to press the bottom plank. The width of this beveled plank can not be given accurately here, because the planed planks are seldom of exact width. But measure carefully from the planks in place to the edge, and make a bevel accordingly. (Fig. 13.)

The other end of the boat is planked in the same way, and then the bottom laid on, beginning at the ends and working towards the center, where a strip of the thirty-seventh plank will probably have to be sawed to fit in. This strip is beveled on both edges and "jumped" into place before nailing.

Now square up the ends of the plank by sawing off the projecting ends.

If the work has been well done with straight planks, and plenty of white lead used, the hull literally will not leak a drop.

Shellac the knots and paint with three coats of paint—red paint is preferred by the river men.

When the hull is dry enough, turn it over. Of course it can be turned over before painting, but it had better have at least one coat before turning over, because then every square inch is thoroughly covered; besides painting the bottom from the underside is a task that tries the back of the neck—and the soul.

In turning over the hull will stand a good deal of racking, but the gentler it is handled, the less likelihood there is of straining it. Four or five men can flop it over, but it is better to have eight or ten men, so that the bottom can be turned down on the horses without shock by mere lifting.

The next things to put in the hull are four timber heads, to which the mooring lines of the boat are to be tied. These are the 42 inch 4 x 4 oak pieces. Having squared them up and planed them, bevel off the edges of one end of each stick. The bevels should extend about half an inch down the sides, all around the top. Then bevel off the corners of the pieces from the top-bevels 11 inches along each edge, to blunt the edges, around which the mooring ropes are to tie, thus preventing chafing the lines.

At the opposite ends of the timber heads a cut must be made to rabbet the posts on the side stringers of the hull. The cut should be 6 inches long and 1½ inches deep (Fig. 14).

The timberheads are then put in place. The two for the stern are placed with one side against the foot of the rake, as near the end of the boat so it will stand flat on the bottom and rabbet firmly to the stringer. Three-eighth inch holes are then bored through the timberhead and the sides of the hull, two holes to each strake, or plank, of the side, except the gunwale, which should have three bolts (Fig. 15).

The bow timberheads are bolted in the same way, but instead of standing at the foot of the rake, they must be placed 3 feet from the inside of the bumper. The reason for this is the oar pinheads which are placed at the foot of the bow rake, and bolted in the same way that the timberheads are. The oar pinheads (32 inches long, 5 x 5 oak) are planed, and beveled off to a round top 4 feet, 10½ inches from the bumper. (See Fig. 16).

In the top of the oar-pin head, sink a half inch hole about a foot. In this drive a $\frac{5}{8}$ inch round iron about 18 inches long, leaving 6 inches projecting above the pinhead.

The next thing is to put in the decks. Notches for the deck timbers must first be cut in the gunwales. In the bow two notches $1\frac{1}{2}$ inches wide are cut 1 foot, 8 inches from the bumper. Two are cut 3 feet, 4 inches from the bumpers. Two are cut 4 feet, $10\frac{1}{2}$ inches from the bumper. (See Fig. 16.)

The deck beams (5-inch wide hemlock plank) are then slipped, edge down, into the notches, claw nailed fast and then the ends sawed off even with the sides of the boat.

In the stern notches, 5 inches deep and $1\frac{1}{2}$ inches wide, are cut in the gunwales, one 2 feet and one 3 feet, $10\frac{1}{2}$ inches from the stern bumper on each gunwale. The deck beams are slipped into place, claw nailed fast and the ends sawed off even with the sides.

Note that the inmost beam from the bow is exactly 5 feet from the bumper to the far side, while the inmost beam of the stern is exactly 4 feet from the stern bumper to the inmost edge.

It is a good plan now to paint the inside of the hull with two coats of barn paint, to save it from decay. Select the best flooring for the decks, cut the tongue off a strip 5 feet, 4 inches long, notch for timber and car pin heads and lay it along the bow gunwale, groove side in. Nail it fast even with the edge. Set home the tongue of another piece of flooring in the groove, with the end flush with the outside of the bumper; nail fast. Saw off even with the deck beam. Repeat. It will make the deck watertight if the grooves of the flooring are white-leaded.

The stern is decked over like the bow, but with 4 feet, 4-inch strips instead of with 5 feet, 4 inch.

In the list of lumber, provision is made for only enough material to make a cabin 6 feet, 4 inches clear between the stringers of the hull and the carlins of the roof. This plan has been followed throughout, but it is worth saying here that the boat builder will do well to consider whether he wants any hold space or not. If he does, he should arrange to raise his floor off the stringers to the desired height. If it is desired, the deck beams can be continued from the bow to the stem, two feet apart. The cabin can be erected with the floor on a level with the decks. This will give more than 400 cubic feet of hold for storing junk, merchandise, produce, etc. Trap doors or hatches in the floor, or decks, give access to the hold.

But if one is not going to carry a cargo, the floor should be set down in the hull, because the boat will not be so stable with no ballast, if the weight of the furniture, stoves and inmates is higher than the top of the gunwales. Moreover, a high cabin catches the wind, and a boat that stands high above the water can not float on days when a low craft will follow the current without undue work at the sweeps. Incidentally, the higher the cabin, the more the material required. The low cabin is here described.

The flooring should now be laid on the stringers, from side to side of the hull. If the ends do not happen to fit close, a mop board 4 or 5 inches wide, can be nailed along on top of the flooring against the side of the hull. In the stern of the cabin on either side— on the same side with the stove, usually—a pump well should be left in the floor. This is simply a hole five or six inches square, in which the cabinboater can see the bottom of his boat, and learn whether there is any water coming in or not. If there is any water, the pump can be worked without going outdoor by discharging through a hole in the cabin side above the gunwale over the well. Sometimes a well is cut in the floor at each end of the cabin, in case the bow should be drawing more than the stern.

With the decks and floor in, the hull is ready for the superstructure—the cabin.

The frame must be built first. The upright stuff is sawed to the proper length—4 feet, 4 inches—of which pieces ten are needed. The plates are sawed to a length of 9 feet, 9 inches, four being required.

The uprights are nailed in place as follows:

One on the inside of the gunwales, with flat side (2 inches) against the bow and stern flooring. The other six are placed amidships, with the center two 5 feet, 4 inches from the bow decking, one on each gunwale; two 9 feet, 4 inches from the decking and two 12 feet, 4 inches from the decking. These uprights are toe-nailed to the gunwales, so that they stand on end. Along the tops of these are nailed the plates, which project beyond the end uprights 3 inches.

The 12 carlins are now nailed in place, 19 inches apart, from center to center, beginning at the bow. Each carlin projects 2 inches over each plate. The two end ones are set flush with the endsides of the bow and stern uprights (Fig. 17).

The struts are now put in place. The struts are sawed in a 45-degree mitre box, and should be about 2 feet long, 2 inches wide and 1 inch thick. They are put in every angle, bracing the uprights from the hull up and from the plates down. They are held in place by 3-inch nails, toe-nailed through the struts into gunwale, upright and plates (see diagram 1).

It is a good plan to chink in the spaces between

the ends of the carlins above the plates with 18-inch sticks, 1½ inch thick, though some cabin boats are chinked under the caves by merely notching the siding.

There is room for choice in putting in the door ways. My own preference is to have the door way next to one or other gunwale, but the usual river boat has the doors in the middle of the bow and stern ends of the cabin. Owing to the height of the decks, the doorways are necessarily low—4 feet 6 inches high.

The frame work at the ends of the cabin consists of four uprights, 2 x 1 inches, and a shade over 6 feet 4 inches long. The shade should be one-eighth of an inch, if the flooring is seven-eighths inch thick. If it is only six-eighths of an inch thick, it would be one-fourth of an inch. One of these uprights is stood on end on the floor with the 2-inch face against the deck timber and under the bow carlin 2 feet 6 inches from the port gunwale; another is placed upright 2 feet 6 inches from the other gunwale. Both are toe-nailed to the carlin and the floor, and nailed to the deck timber. The same is done with the other uprights at the stern. These uprights are braced by struts 2 feet long, 2 inches wide and 1 inch thick, sawed wide side down in a 45-degree mitre box. The braces are put in between the two uprights, against the carlin, one against each upright, as shown in diagram 2.

The frame is now ready to board up. One must now consider where the windows are to be placed, and the kinds of windows that will be put in. The more windows there are, the more cheerful the boat on dark days.

Cut off the groove of one tier of the siding and lay it against the upright on the gunwale and nail fast.

The groove is cut off because the thin lips are likely to split and leave a crack through which the wind and water may drive. Spaces for the windows are left when building up the sides. At the top of the sides, a line of notched siding fits on the carlin completely filling the space to the tops of the carlins. The ends of the cabin boat are built up in the same way, from the top of the decking to the top of the carlin, the curve being cut in the siding with a draw knife. Of course, space for the window and door is left at each end of the boat.

When the sides are on, lay on the roof, beginning by shaving off the grooved side of a piece of siding and nailing along the tops of the carlins at the extreme ends. In laying the roof planking it is a good plan to daub the grooves of the matched stuff with white lead. When the whole top has been covered, either canvas or roofing paper should be laid on. If canvas is used, paint the roof first, and sew up the breadths to lie the short way, and lay the canvas on in a big sheet, like a carpet. Tack it firmly on the edges of the roof planking—a copper tack every two inches. Paint the canvas with several coats of thin outside paint—white is the usual color for the roof. If roofing paper is used, it is a good plan to paint the boat and then lay the paper on, laying the side sheets first and overlapping with the next strip, and finally having the middle strip overlap the two adjoining ones.

In putting in the windows, ready made casings and frames are purchased. The door jambs are made $\frac{3}{4}$ inch thick, $2\frac{1}{2}$ inch wide planed wood. The door should be made to open toward the inside. The jambs are fitted in first. The height from the deck to the underside of the carlin is measured—it will be about

4 feet 5 inches. Then make a T lap of the jambs, so the door will close against a half inch strip of solid wood. (Fig. 18).

Two of these jambs are fitted in place, one on each side of the doorway. The lintel is laid against the carlin, after being sawed and draw-knifed to fit. The other doorway is fitted in the same way.

Then on all four outside corners of the cabin are fitted mouldings from gunwales to the roof. Along the top of the two gunwales, against the siding, are laid quarter-round strips ⅝ inch on a side. These strips, carefully daubed with white lead, are securely bradded in place, giving additional protection against the wind and waves.

Steps from the deck to the cabin floor must be made at each door. Two pieces on which to rest the steps must be cut out for each pair of steps.

The figure indicates the shape of the step supports. The square is laid on a board a foot wide so that one leg reads 7 inches and the other 11 inches from the same edge of the board. From the edge of the 7-inch line, another line 11 inches long is drawn on the board. From the inside end of this 11-inch board a perpendicular is drawn to the opposite side of the board. Perpendicular from the end of the first 11-inch line a line 7 inches long is drawn on the board. From the end of this 7-inch line, another perpendicular is drawn to the opposite edge of the board. (Fig. 19).

Four pieces of this size and shape must be cut for the two pairs of steps.

Boards for the steps must be cut—two 11 inches wide, two 7 inches wide for each pair. These boards are cut about 2 feet 8 inches long and the two upper 11-inch and 7-inch ones must be fitted into the doorway, against the upright and flooring. The step supports are nailed against the side of the boat and against the upright. The one against the upright rests with one side against the inside of a cleat on the floor, 2 feet 6 inches from the gunwale. (See Fig. 20).

The doors consist of strips of flooring about 4 feet 6 inches long, with cleats across the back (inside). The groove and tongue of the outside edges are planed off and the hinges set about a foot from top and bottom, against the gunwale jamb.

Holes are now cut for the stovepipes. Some cabinboaters prefer to have the chimney stick out the side of the boat. Usually the pipe goes straight up from the stove through the roof. Wherever the pipes are placed, be sure that there is at least three inches of iron or zinc between the pipe and the wood around it.

The boat can now be used as a floating home or camp, but a partition will add materially to the comfort and coziness of the craft. Where the partition is placed depends on whether a large kitchen and small front room, or vice versa, are desired. The partition adds to the strength of the cabin—something worth considering where the winds blow 80 miles an hour on occasions.

Two uprights are dropped from a carlin to the floor, nailed and toe-nailed fast 2 feet 6 inches apart, and opposite cabin uprights in the side of the boat. On the gunwales and hull uprights must also be nailed to give backing for the siding used to board up the partition. A door can be fitted in, or one can use a heavy curtain to cut the rooms off from each other.

One thing more remains to be done—close up the openings under the decks. This is easily done by simple upright siding, nailed against the deck beams and against a strip of 2 x 1½-inch stuff nailed on the stringers or projecting ends of the cabin flooring for backing. As this space under the decks is likely to be useful for storing odds and ends, a trap door might be fitted, giving access to the space. Boards laid on the stringers will keep everything under the decks off the bottom.

Now bolt two iron cleats, 9 inches long, to the bow and stern bumpers midway from the ends. The bow cleat is to hold the gangplank when it is serving as a spar, and the stern cleat is to serve to hold the anchor line, skiff, painter, etc. Because of these cleats, it is necessary to strap the bow and stern bumpers to the gunwales.

Last of all, fit footlogs, an inch high all around the edges of the decks, over bumpers and gunwales. Here and there leave scuppers two inches wide, to let the water run off the deck. The footlogs will serve to stop a slipping foot, and save one from a ducking. If little children are aboard, railings must be provided of course.

Now paint everything inside and out—paint with good paint, and several coats on the outside at least. Paint the inside white or some other light, cheerful color.

When the boat is dry, hitch an inch line to one of the timberheads and slide it on skids down the bank into the river. It is then ready for fitting and furnishing.

OTHER CABIN BOATS.

In the previous pages, a complete cabin boat was described in detail. The idea in going into details was to enable any one to follow out the instructions and make for himself a boat fit to live in the year around, during a number of years. The construction of the hull was, as said, along the usual lines of the Mississippi shanty-boat. The sides were four inches thick at the bottom strake. This was because the shanty-boaters found their boats compelled to resist the blows and the pressure of drift and ice, but in recent years, the tendency has been to build the boats of two inch, or even less, sides and bottom. The saving in work is considerable, and the saving in cost of materials is also noticeable. Moreover, the boat is considerably lighter in weight, and is easier to handle with oars.

This boat is made a good deal lighter in the hull, by the simple expedient of having all the strakes of the hull made of two-inch plank, or even $1\frac{1}{2}$-inch plank, instead of having the heavy four inch thick timbers. This will make the cabin boat hull four inches narrow, for which the bottom plank must be sawed. By using matched heavy planking, say four inches wide, a fine bottom and sides can be made, and the weight will be very much less; the boat will handle easier, too. But of course, the gain is offset in some measure by the thinner sides being less able to resist crushing strains. The advantages on the ice-bound stream are with the heavy bottom, and the advantages are with the light boat in open river waters, where there is little or no drift.

By care in making landings and seeking shelter in time of runouts there is no reason why the light hull would not serve. It all depends.

Something should be said about the make-shift boats that one may make if he sets out to do it. Mere hints should be sufficient to outdoor men in this devising of cabin-boat and rag-boat shelters. Opposite

Painted Cloth Cover for a Skiff.

Hickman, Ky., I saw a man putting a roof over a large skiff—just an ordinary fisherman's skiff, about twenty feet long. He was making a little cabin, about three and a half feet high, and eight feet long. By spreading down his mattress and blankets, he was sure of a dry bed, at least. Only, of course, he had to cover the open bow of the boat with waterproof canvas, when it rained to prevent the water filling the hull, and flowing aft into the cabin.

Just an ordinary scow hull—cabin boat hull of small size, made of inch or inch and a half planks, and water tight, twenty feet long, five feet wide, and eighteen or twenty inches deep, decked over and cabined with either a frame and roofing material, or even mere tar paper, laid on thin boards; one could put up a tent on a frame on such a scow. The cost would not be great—that is all that is needed for a most primitive kind of a houseboat. Such an outfit, fit for a trip down thousands of miles of river, costs no more than a small tent, and it handles almost as easily as a skiff. For one or two young men, of good natures and well experienced, there is hardly any river in the Mississippi Basin but what could be traveled in this little house-on-a-boat.

To these I may add suggestions by other cabin-boaters:

House Boat.

I will give the build and size of my house boat. In the first place I build two scows out of one-inch pine boards with one and one-fourth pine for the sides $1\frac{1}{4}$ x 12, 16 feet long and cut the one-inch boards three feet long and nail on crosswise. Calk and make water tight.

Have two of these scows and have them four feet apart and floor over with 1 x 10, 10 feet long clear across the two scows. Then you have your house floor. Build your house frame with 2 x 2 and cover sides with ⅜ ceiling. On roof cover with ½-inch boards, then tar paper, then put ½-inch boards over paper again to protect frame from storm. Two thicknesses of paper will last for years. Your roof only needs about eight inch crown, so you can spring the boards down to the side plates. It is what we call a car roof out here. All that is needed is a 2 x 8 for ridge and 2 x 2 for plates. No rafters, just post to hold up end of ridge piece.

The house would be 10 x 10 square, leaving three feet at each end for deck, which should be calked tight with hatch holds so you could keep things down in the boat. A lot of things could be stored in that way that were not in use. I have a small cook stove which weighs about sixty pounds and granite dishes of all kinds, cups, saucers, plates and all, granite being light. My bunks are wire spring cots with one side fastened to the wall with strap hinges so you can turn up against the wall when not in use. Table top is hinged against the wall with two legs that swing out to place when the table is let down, with all complete and ready for business. The boats only draw about five inches of water and are easier to pull against the current than one single scow for the same size house. This is for all complete, grub, axes, traps and all on board.

ANOTHER HOUSE BOAT.

I see in the H-T-T the lone trapper of Arkansas wants to know how to build a house boat with a six by twelve cab on it. I lived in house boats for nine years and have built about twenty, all of different styles and I certainly have a fine one now. I live in it the year round. I hunt, trap and fish, don't do any work at all and have a good time on the old Rock River, Ill. I will tell the lone trapper of Arkansas how to build his boat.

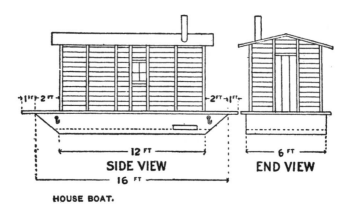

HOUSE BOAT.

Make the scow six feet wide and sixteen feet long, eighteen inches high. Use two-inch plank, twelve inches wide. Put scow together with pitch. Build cab of flooring and put a car roof on. Put floor four inches from scow bottom as shown in figure and a small window in each. Let boards extend out over scow one foot so as to make a three-foot platform on each end and the boat will go along nicely loaded with 500 pounds in eight inches of water. Tar paper is all right for roof. Put door in each end.

Make cot so that it can be put up on side of boat on hinges, as it will make lots more room in day time.

Shacks on Rafts.

Mention should be made of the rafts that are used by the people in the overflow lands and by the loggers of the mountain country east of the Mississipi and south of the Ohio. Many of the bottom lands people in danger of overflow have log rafts nearby for stock and for their own safety, should the water get too high to live in their houses.

The first man to live on Reelfoot lake had a log raft with a house built on it, and he had a hole in the floor of the cabin through which he caught fish for himself and to sell to river steamers which landed at Tiptonville, a few miles distant. Moreover, he trapped and sold meat of wild game to the people at New Madrid.

The log raft is even used for traveling, and I came down the Tennessee and Holston rivers several hundred miles on rafts. On these rafts were built little shacks in which the logger crews lived in making their trip with the logs from the timber land to the saw mills.

Where one has a lake and wishes to move from place to place, but cannot make a cabin-boat, dry log poles bound together by wire or poles or poles-and-pins, and chinked up will serve for the foundation of a good little cabin, or a tent. On the St. Francis river the most efficient trappers usually had log rafts with cabins on them, using dugouts or skiffs to work up and down the water lines, and they were safe from overflow. If they desired—and many did so desire—they could float down the river hundreds of miles, trapping a locality a few days and then dropping down the river to another ground and trapping there.

6 C. B. P.

At the Grub Boxes on a Log Raft.

Of course, the log raft is merely a substitute for a cabin-boat, but it is a most efficient substitute especially where one could not build a house-boat without great or prohibitive expense. People who live much by the water will do well to bear in mind all the cabin-boat variations, from the mere skiff, housed in at night by a sheet of canvas to the cabin cruiser, log raft shack, tar-paper boat, rag-cabin, and scow hull or model hull cabin boat.

A development of the log raft is found in the catamaran or "double hull" boat. Two large pine logs, well dried, with joists reaching from log to log, holding them ten feet apart, and floored was probably the original of the Mississippi river two-hull boats. Then came some one who took two skiffs or narrow scows and planked them over and put on a cabin. Once in a while now one comes across a shantyboat with two hulls put side by side and decked over, with a cabin on the deck. There is little advantage gained by the two-hull idea, except that a very light construction can be devised, and use can be made of two hulls in making one good sized cabin room.

CHAPTER V.

The Cabin Boat's Equipment.

ONE must have oars or sweeps, with which to row the boat across the current to the bank, or out of eddies.

For making a pair of sweeps, four straight grained boards, pine preferably, 12 feet long, 3 inches wide, and 1 inch thick; two boards 30 inches long 6 inches wide and $1\frac{1}{2}$ inches thick, and four pieces of white oak 18 inches long, 3 inches wide, 2 inches thick are necessary.

The boards are all planed carefully. Then one end of each of the long boards is cut off diagonally from the end on one edge to a point one foot from the end of the opposite edge (Fig. 1).

One of the 18-inch oak sticks is smoothed off, and a hole $\frac{5}{8}$ inch in diameter is bored 9 inches from the ends through the center line on the 2 x 18 face. This hole is reamed out on top and bottom to a width of 1 inch and a depth of $1\frac{1}{2}$ inch, the cone terminating at a depth of $1\frac{1}{2}$ inch from each side at the $\frac{5}{8}$-inch center (Fig. 2).

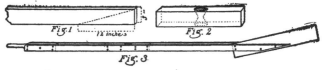

This block is bolted with eight 4 $\frac{1}{2}$-$\frac{1}{4}$ inch bolts and washers between two twelve foot boards so that the hole is $4\frac{1}{2}$ feet from the square ends of the 12-foot boards.

Then another of the 18-inch pieces is smoothed
off and a handle whittled six inches long on one end.
This handle should be very smooth—well sandpapered
—and about 2 inches in diameter. This block is fitted
between the "square ends" of the two boards, with
the handle projecting, and bolted with five 4½ in. ¼ in.
bolts. (Fig. 3).

Now one of the 30-inch boards is planed to a
thickness of ¾ of an inch at one end for a blade. This
board is bolted between the diagonal ends of the two
boards so that the upper 1½-inch corner is level with
the top of the two boards, and the diagonal board
edges quarter of an inch from the bottom of the blade.
(Fig. 3). The boards are then bolted together with
four 4-inch ¼-inch bolt. When the sweep—all but
the handle—has been painted it is ready for business.
Two sweeps are required.

For making fast to the bank, four lines are necessary. For the 28-foot boat, ¾-inch ropes are large
enough. The ropes that run to the stern timberheads should be 75 feet long and the two bow ropes
should be 40 feet long. In the chapter on "Making
Fast and Some Rope Hints" will be found directions
for the use of the mooring lines.

A gang plank should be made 9 feet 6 inches
long, 10 inches wide and 2 inches thick. Near one
end bore an inch-hole and take a seven-foot length
of inch rope and thread it through the hole, knotting
both ends of the rope so that it can not get out of
the hole. The plank is kept across the bow, against
the cleat on the bumper, to which the rope is always
kept tied save when taking the plank in or out.

A handy line, as its name implies, is one of the
most useful ropes on a boat. A half-inch rope from
150 to 500 feet long is a proper handy line for a 28-

foot cabinboat.   The Sunny South, a noted Ohio river 90-foot store boat has a handy line 3,000 feet long and an inch and a half in diameter.   The use of the handy line is described in the chapter on "Making Fast", etc.

An inch line 100 feet long for the anchor should be carried.   Double blocks for use with the handy line are sometimes useful, especially if, for any reason, one wants to beach his boat—or get it off a sand bar.

A 16-foot pike pole—a round pole with a hook and spike at the large end—is most useful, for with it one can recover a hat blown overboard, a camera sunk in the mud, hook a log, lift a line off a stake, or pole the boat into deep water.   The pole should be hung on brackets on the side of the cabin—if two poles are carried, one should be 10 or 12 feet long, and hung on the other side of the cabin.

A lantern that will not blow out is absolutely necessary.   It should burn oil, hang on its own hook indoors where it can be found at any time of the night.   By its side matches should be hung in a safe. In time of night trouble, the first thing to do is to get a light.

An acetylene lamp, throwing a beam of light 100 yards or more is very useful.   For boatwork, an automobile headlight serves to pick out a landing at night and it will show a coon's eyes from afar. If one has a gasoline launch for tender, the large acetylene lamp is servicable as a search light, especially when running narrow chutes in the night.   Of course on wide waters a light is of little value to the pilot. An ax, hammer, brace and bits—including an extension bit—saw and square are well nigh indispensable to the cabinboater.   The tools should be kept oiled, to save from rusting, in a tool box where they can always be found. A jack plane, or smoothing plane, is sometimes servicable, especially in repairing damage to the cabin, putting in partitions or changing fixtures, and putting up mosquito bars.

Once in a while a cabinboater will be able to use a sail on his craft. The ordinary type is a big square sheet bent on two square yards and a perpendicular mast. Used in conjunction with a power launch, or motor on the boat, such a sail aids very much in upstream work before the wind. The mast is simply a long pole, stepped from the bow deck, braced by an iron hoop at the cabin roof, and rising as high as desired into the air. One could use a triangular sail on such a mast, of course.

If one uses a sail, a pin is put in the middle of the stern bumper, from which one of the oars, or a sweep rudder is hung, to steer the boat. A sail in proportion to the size of the boat, is certainly of great service in still waters, or in going against the current.

A stage plank on which to walk from the boat to the shore is necessary. It should be a light, stiff board, ten feet long, or thereabouts. Through one end is bored an inch auger hole. In this hole is knotted an inch line, about five or six feet long. One end of the board is placed against a stake on the bank, and the other on the boat, and the rope, fastened to a cleat in the middle of the bow bumper, holds the boat off the bank. See "Making Fast" and "Rope Hints".

An anchor, or even two anchors, are of prime importance. Many cabinboats do not have them; nevertheless, few things in a boat's equipment are more serviceable. The weight depends on the size of the boat. Ten pounds will hold a pretty large skiff, and a forty-pound anchor with wide "mud hooks" for flukes, will serve for a 30-foot cabinboat. An anchor does very well to hold a boat against the bank, as well as off it.

There should always be something on board that will serve for a sea anchor. When caught in a gale of wind, it is essential to keep off the bank, or gain time before hitting. The stageplank, held perpendicular to the surface of the water by ropes, will serve for a sea anchor and a half pork barrel, used for a washtub, ordinarily and easily slung in a rope pocket and dropped overboard astern, will check the speed of a boat headed for land before a gale. Incidentally, a sea anchor will tow a boat down stream on a windy day, when progress would otherwise be impossible.

Be sure and have a good pump with which to pump out the hold in case of leak or water coming over the side through the doors. A pump is not expensive and it is far and away better than bailing with a pail.

Enough life preservers to go around, and a buoy with a long rope attached to it, to throw in case of "Man overboard" are good life insurance, seldom seen on the river shantyboats, however, though compulsory now on motorboats, and becoming more and more frequent in river equipments.

CHAPTER VI.

FURNISHINGS AND FURNITURE.

WHAT one carries in the boat will depend on the object of the trip, the size of the boat and the taste of the cabin boater. The necessities are stove, table, chairs and bed.

The bed can be made folding like a sleeping car upper berth. Heavy hinges let down a long, narrow box full of bedding—and a straw or cotton mattress. If it is close to the floor, two legs drop down for the bunk to rest on. If close to the roof, two pieces of rope or light chain support the outer edge from catlins overhead. If the boat is large enough, bedsteads are sometimes introduced. Light, folding cots are very satisfactory for comfortable sleeping. Especial care should be taken that the sleeping arrangements are comfortable. Even in Louisiana, there are nights in winter when ample bedding is needful.

A cupboard in the kitchen, or kitchen end of the boat to hold all the dishes, including pans and kettles, is useful. Fix it so that waves will not jump the things out, or throw open the door. This is done with cleats or little compartments for plates, cups, etc., and wooden buttons or latches on doors. In the opposite corner, another cupboard for eatables should be put up, with several shelves. Outside in the stern some kind of a cooler for meats, and the like should be arranged; a dry goods box, with a door and shelves, nailed fast, serves well. It should, of course, be impervious to rain.

An oil stove saves a vast deal of trouble. On its own table or legs, burning fuel that doesn't need splitting or tiresome journeys to drift piles, and requiring no dirty wood box, but instead only a movable can, the oil stove has advantages unmistakable, though it is much more expensive as far as money is concerned than wood and the cabin boaters, most of them, use wood. The tyro will learn that all woods do not burn alike; that dry wood is better than wet, and that ash, dry willow, oak pine, etc., etc., are what he wants to get. A few sticks of dry cedar for shavings and a few splinters of dry pine for kindlings, will start most drift wood burning, providing it is not saturated. The stove for cooking is very small, taking twelve or fourteen inch sticks. An oven is indispensable, whether for blue flame oil stove, or wood stove. A heater is often carried as well as a cook stove. Because one can pick up coal on many sand bars, stoves that take either wood or soft coal should be taken down the Ohio or Mississippi. If the boat is well built, tight and small, one stove is ample. An oil stove with yellow flame burns about two gallons a week cooking meals, a blue flame rather less. If used for heating it might take two quarts or more a day, but with warm days and merely cool evenings, the amount burned is less. A common heater oil stove in a small boat would make it warm enough. A five-gallon oil can, or a woodbox and storage capacity for half a cord or more of wood should be provided. It's a long ways between drift piles and stores on a cabinboat journey.

A table on legs, or hanging like a bed bunk, serves as a dining table, but a little table by the stove for holding things at meal cooking time is useful. Camp stools are economical of space, but they try the temper. It is much better to have comfortable chairs of wood, or even rattan than to lose one's temper over boxes and stools. For a cabinboat journey, or living, one should go to some trouble and even expense to secure comfort, the prime requisite of proper cabinboat life.

Lamps should have broad bases and stand low upon table, or cleated shelf. A lamp with a high standard is almost sure to upset in rough weather. A hanging lamp, or ship's lamp, makes a pleasant reading light, but it should have a table under it, for the ceiling is low, and one is likely to bump into it and break a chimney, far from a store.

If one wishes, a fibre or straw matting for carpet adds to a boat's comfort but it is sure to get muddy. Ordinarily, the bare floor serves the hunting outfit to better advantage, and a mop should not be forgotten. A box of dry sand, or saw dust, to sprinkle on the floor before sweeping "cuts" the dirt.

If the journey is undertaken for a period when flies and mosquitoes are abroad, the windows must surely be covered with netting.

Curtains over the windows add to the boat's good looks, and at night add to the feeling of security from intrusive gaze. "You never know who's looking in," the cabin boater says as he pulls down the shades at dusk.

A shelf for books and papers, or even a writing desk of cheap make, goes far toward making the keeping of notes, the writing of letters and the like, easier to do. It is worth while to work hard preparing for days of indolent comfort. Each builder of a houseboat, or outfitter of a boat will do well to think what his own particular longings or intentions are, and then, with due regard to proportion, fit out for them. It should not be forgotten that cabinboat life brings out the true inwardness of a man's nature, and to meet that nature's desires is a potential reason for cabin boating.

The arrangement of the boat must be left to the taste of the outfitter. The cooking is usually done in the stern of the cabin, the bunk is on the diagonally opposite side from the stove and woodpile, to balance, and everything is distributed so as to keep the boat on an even keel, and down at the stern rather than at the bow, when in motion.

A box for the handy line, a gun rack, a closet for hanging up clothes, a box for boots and shoes, a trough for odds and ends along one or the other side of the boat at the top of the wainscoting, a partition between the kitchen and the bow cabin, a reclining chair, a dark room and a developing sink, with barrel for clear or rain water with which to develop and wash pictures—these are hints. The mere hunter, the mere fisherman, the trader, has each his own particular needs, as gunracks and ammunition cases, net boxes, goods counters, and shelves. The traveler, having camera guns and fishing tackle, must needs think how best to arrange his things for his own purpose—and the planning of an hour may make the difference between a joyous experience and an uncomfortable existence.

A work table should be made, if one has a motor towboat or has a motorcycle or bicycle on board. Make the table of a wide, two-inch plank, and have a good iron vise, which does not cost much, but holds wood or metal for working.

Under Skiff and Tender, discussion of bicycle and motorcycle is had, briefly. I never missed my bicycle more than when I was on shantyboats, and lately, now that I have a motorcycle, I see possibilities in that for all kinds of out-door people.

I saw one shanty-boater who kept his bicycle hung to the side of the cabin on brackets, the handle bars being turned so it would hang close; and straps holding the frame taut to the wall, so it would not swing and pound. The man used it in riding out on the bottoms to sell pictures and trinkets in which he dealt. He could cover five times as much ground as a man on foot, if the roads were in any kind of condition. I have seen in the last two or three years, a number of motorboats which carried light automobiles, and a number of power house boats have been built with automobile garage, and the shanty-boat might very well have place for the poor man's bicycle or motorcycle. There is plenty of country near cabin boating waters where the hunter, trapper and fisherman might increase his sport and his profit by using a bicycle and motorcycle.

CHAPTER VII.

ODDS AND ENDS OF EQUIPMENT.

THERE are many small articles of value to the cabin boater, sooner or later. A mere list of them will serve to suggest to the cabin boater useful things to have along:

A good, big Jackknife.

A first class compass.

Gloves, mittens.

Acetylene lamp—automobile size.

A headlamp for coon, 'possum or other night hunting.

Slippers for boat wear.

Wash basin.

Hip boots, rubber.

Sewing kit, containing needles, thread, thimble, emery, beeswax, shoemaker's wax, sail needle, sailor's palm patches, buttons, etc., etc.

Turkey and duck calls. (See "Hunting.")

Traps.

Nails.

Wire for snares, etc.

Camera (See "Photographing").

String, stout net twine. A pound or two is most useful. It should be rolled on a reel, or at least into a ball, and kept in a box or on the wall, handy for its thousand services.

Cloth bags for sugar, oatmeal, odds and ends, etc.

Long boxes, divided into compartments for ammunition, tackle, nails, tools trinkets and what not can be put in along the wall behind the doors, or under the bed, or even in the hold of a boat that does not leak.

It is always a good idea for the hunter and outdoor man, about to undertake a trip, to write down all the things he thinks he would be likely to need. Such a list should be divided into parts, as the camping outfit, the clothes, the food supply, the sporting implements, and everything that might be used should be written down. With such a list before him, the camper out is not apt to arrive at his hunting country and find that he had forgotten his ammunition, or his moccasins, or some other part of his equipment. If one has the list of articles which he carried on two or three trips, he will have a very complete record of his needs and desires. In nothing is the list more important than in this one of odds and ends.

CHAPTER VIII.

The Skiff or Tender.

NO one should go afloat in a house boat without a tender. The stranger to river life especially should be sure to have a good stout skiff tied to his cabin-boat. Then if the cabin-boat sinks, one can at least get ashore.

For light running around, nothing is better than a 16 or 18-foot clinker built skiff, but if one intends to fish or to drift (catch logs) for money, a heavier boat is better.

If one can afford to have a little gasoline launch beside the cabinboat, great will be the pleasure he will derive from it. With a two-horsepower engine in a row boat the 25-foot cabinboat can be towed hither and yon, up bayous and through eddies and to and from landings disregarding all but the cyclonic gales that sometimes sweep over the Mississippi. Of course the more horsepower in a boat, the more one can tow with it and if one aims to catch logs and make money, a gasoline launch of staunch build is as good an investment as one can make.

Rafts, of astonishing size, can be rescued from the drift and brought ashore with a small launch of two or three horsepower. Gasoline engines use about a gallon a day per horsepower and alcohol engines will be less expensive than gasoline at the rate of 20 cents a gallon or more. Gasoline is sometimes cheaper in the South than in the North. See "The Gasoline Launch".

The skiff's oars should be leathered where the shaft comes in the locks and the end should be coppered or tinned. A piece of leather eight inches long and just wide enough to wrap around the oar without lapping should be tacked on. Then at the handle end of the leather, a "collar" of a long leather strap, or short leather strips should be tacked on, so that the oar will not slip down through the lock into the water. A tinsmith will put on the tin or copper tips for half a dollar. Heavy tin or copper should be used.

A cabin and a good lock are necessary parts of a skiff's equipment, for river thieves will steal a good skiff at the first opportunity. At a landing, where there is wind blowing, it is always a good plan to draw the skiff up on the bank, clear of the water. Failure to do this may result in losing the boat; in any event, it would be swamped. Of course, davits on the cabin boat would do better.

The oars are kept indoors or strapped to the cabin boat roof. A sponge and scoop for bailing are necessary. A good seat mat can be made of old rope, coiled around and around and sewed with twine and a sailor's needle.

A sail on the skiff will sometimes be the means of plenty of sport, or save arm work at the oars. A rawhide loop at the stern for using an oar as a rudder is helpful in steering.

Many cabinboaters use log canoes on the river for small river work—as up the White, Hatchie, Obion, etc., etc. A light canoe will certainly be a joy to the paddle lovers. In any houseboat waters, a canoe would add to the pleasure of the trip.

A hunter will perhaps want a sneakbox in which to approach ducks and geese. Some market hunters on the Mississippi travel in a 16-foot launch and tow

7 C. B. P.

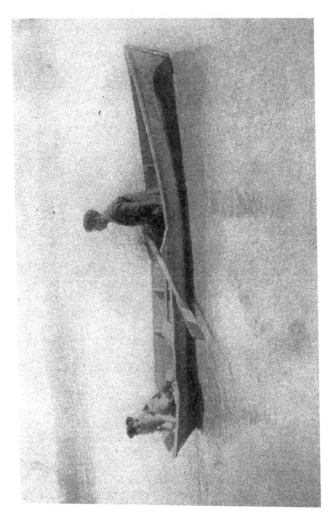

A Good Tennessee River Skiff.

a sneakbox to their hunting grounds. A launch and one other boat is about all one would care to have tied to a cabinboat, but of course a light canoe could be lashed to the roof of the cabin if desired.

To these suggestions I add descriptions of boats which appear to be of particular value under various conditions and for various needs, as follows:

ROUGH AND READY BOAT.

While the boat constructed after the directions below is hardly stylish or very speedy it is serviceable, strong and safe and the cost is so little that a single season or even a few weeks use will repay the builder for all trouble and expense incurred. The material needed is as follows:

BILL OF MATERIAL.

4 boards, 1 ft. wide, inch thick, 16 ft. long, at 3 cents per ft....................	$1.92
1 piece timber, 4 x 6 in., 1 ft. long......	.10
5 lbs. 10d nails at 4 cents per lb..........	.20
10 lbs. pitch at 1½ cents per lb..........	.15
Total.........................	$2.37

The boards may be rough hemlock or pine, and should have no loose knots; two of them should have no large knots or cracks.

The boat will have a better appearance if the boards are dressed but that is not essential.

For the sides of the bateau use the two best boards, first cutting them down to twelve feet in length. Make a mark six inches from the end of one of them and saw it across diagonally, this is the bow end.

If the Same at Bow as Stern, Would be a Jon-Boat.

Mark nine inches down the diagonal cut and two feet six inches back from the lower end and connect these marks by a saw cut. This takes off a long wedge shaped piece and makes the upward curve of the bottom at the bow.

Mark nine inches down the stem end, which is square and two feet along the lower edge, sawing off another wedge not quite as large as before. This curves the bottom up at the stern. Laying this board on the one selected for the other side it is an easy matter to mark and saw it.

Next saw or hew the four by six piece in the shape of a triangle, minus the apex. The base of the triangle should be five and one-half inches and the opposite side should have a width of two inches.

Lay this on one of the side boards at the bow, mark the slant of the bottom and saw the end of the bow post off.

Now the sides may be nailed securely to this post, being sure to get them even with the two-inch face of it.

Another board should be ripped into two pieces one nine inches wide, the other three of course, and a piece two feet long cut from the nine-inch piece. A stick or piece of board three feet long placed midway of the side boards will hold them the proper distance apart while bending them till able to nail them to the stern board just cut.

If the boards are wet they will bend easier and with less danger of breaking, though unless assisted by a second person the workman will be obliged to use a rope or strap to draw them together and hold them until they can be nailed. Another nine-inch piece

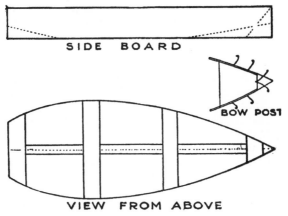

SIDE BOARD

BOW POST

VIEW FROM ABOVE

must be nailed across on top of stern and sides forming the stern seat and holding the sides firmly together. Boards may now be laid across the bottom, marked, sawed and nailed on until the bow is reached.

Use about four nails in the end of each board and see that the pieces are close together, leaving no large cracks.

Two pieces of the nine-inch board are sawed to use as seats, the remainder may be used with the wider pieces in making the boat bottom.

One of these seats should be fitted about three feet from the stern and the other two feet ahead of the middle. The ends should rest on cleats nailed to the side boards and the seats firmly nailed in place as they brace the boat and prevent the sides from springing. A triangular strip should be fitted over the bow post, (one of the corners of that post, which was ripped off will do) and when fastened on extends down over the bottom board and covers the ends of the side pieces, forming a blunt cut-water. Every hunter has of course a stock of hemp or oakum and the cracks between the bottom boards must be caulked with these, using a hard wood wedge or a dull chisel to drive it into the crevices firmly. Cotton waste will also answer for caulking material.

If the center brace is removed, seats fitted, all cracks and nail holes plugged, the pitch may be got ready for application.

This substance, such as is used on roofs, walls, etc., may be melted in some old iron pot until it can be applied with a swab.

It is well first to take an old tin can and in sailor parlance "pay" the seams with melted pitch, that is pour a thin stream of the stuff along the cracks where it will penetrate the oakum and harden, effectually excluding the water. With the swab smear both inside and out of the boat bottom and your "bateau" is ready for the water.

Oar locks and oars may be used but the hunter will find paddles preferable often, as they enable him to face the bow.

As the craft draws but a few inches of water it may be used on marshes where a shoving pole will be most useful in propelling it.

The bateau constructed as above will easily carry three or four persons and with paint and better lumber is quite as good as any boat of similar character for pleasure riding, fishing, hunting or trapping.

The cost is so low that if only used for one season it can be turned adrift or given away with little loss.

The material can be procured almost anywhere,

Anyone Can Build a Boat and go Traveling.

the pitch being most difficult to obtain, but it is kept by most dealers in building supplies and all ship chandlers.

In case the boat is constructed of a good quality of lumber for considerable use it would be advisable to put in a batten the length of the bottom inside the boat. This should be a piece of board about six inches wide and half an inch thick and it may require some saw cuts to make possible the necessary bending to fit the different angles of the bottom. If this batten is well nailed with about four wire shingle nails to each bottom board and their points clinched (before pitching of course), it will prevent them springing off and add to the durability of the craft.

CANVAS CANOE.

A light portable canoe is very desirable to most hunters and trappers, in many cases necessary to profitable work in their busy season. Also the cost must not be too much. I will endeavor to give the details of constructing such a canoe, 9½ ft. long and 36 in. wide, weighing 35 lbs. and carrying two men or one man and outfit easily. The material used cost about $3.00 and is as follows: 1 12-in. board, 10 ft. long and 1 in. thick; 1 piece of plank 3 ft. long, 1½ x 1½; 7 yds. 8 oz. duck; 3 boxes carpet tacks; 2 doz. 2-in. wood screws; 1 lb. 3d lath nails; a few 8d wire nails; 1 gal. boiled linseed oil; 5 lbs. ochre; 3 lbs. white lead; 60 strips 3 in. wide 26 in. long and ⅛ in. thick. With the above and a saw, hatchet, knife, draw-knife, screw-driver and paint brush the canoe can be built in about one and a half days. The thin strips for use as ribs, were furnished by two old vegetable barrels, but if they are not to be had flat barrel hoops or thin basket stuff of any kind will do.

First put these strips soaking so they will bend easily when we want to bend the ribs into place. Mark and rip off 2 strips 1 in. wide for gunwales, 2 strips ¼ in. wide to go outside these and one piece 1½ in. wide for keel. This leaves the board about 8 in. wide. Cut this board off 8½ ft. long and rip 2 triangular pieces off each so that it will taper from full width (8 in.) 2 ft. from each end to 1½ in. at the ends. Cut these from pieces of 1½-in. plank, and as they should project 6 in. over the end of the keel, board at the heighth of 12 in. from the same; the proper cut for the ends may be found by laying it across a square as 6 and 12 inches from the angle. Fasten these to the keel board with a couple of screws and a nail or two. Two thwarts 2 in. wide and 2 ft. long are cut out and nailed on the ends of two stays, 11 in. long in T shape. These Ts are nailed to the keel board where it begins to taper at each end; 4½ ft. apart. Tie a temporary thwart 34 in. long in middle of the gunwales and drawing the ends together at bow and stern posts, cut the wales off at a long bevel to fit posts.

Nail the gunwales to the posts and the ends of the two permanent thwarts and also give them a few turns of tough wire to prevent the nails from drawing. We are now ready for the ribs. If long enough they may extend from one gunwale to the other and be nailed to the keel board in the middle, but the strips I used were only 26 in. long, requiring two for each rib. These ribs are nailed to the top of the keel board and the outside of the gunwales with 3d nails, close together in the middle of the canoe and slightly separated at each end, more at the gunwale than at the keel, to allow for the greater length of the top of the canoe.

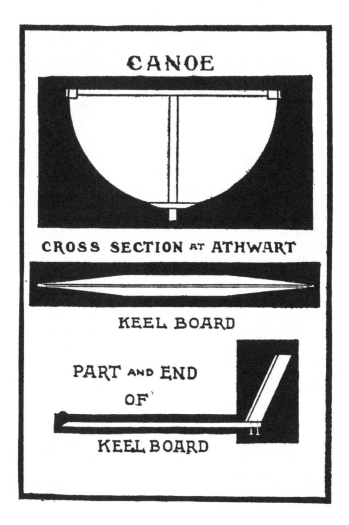

CANOE

CROSS SECTION AT ATHWART

KEEL BOARD

PART AND END OF

KEEL BOARD

The builder should use care to get a good curve on the ribs and to make the sides evenly matched. To begin in the middle and work each way alternately is the best plan. With the ribs the canoe frame is complete and ready for covering.

The duck or canvas is in two pieces each 10½ ft. long, and as it is usually 29 in. wide it is necessary to lap these strips an inch and tack this lap down in the center of the keel board, having turned the canoe frame upside down first. If the canvas is sewed together by hand or machine first it will be easier to handle. Beginning at the middle draw the canvas tight and tack to the gunwales, first on one side, then on the other, until the posts are reached. Draw the canvas snugly over the posts, lapping one side over the other and tacking it securely. Lay the keel right over the seam and screw it to keel board, countersinking the screw heads; cover the joining on the posts with pieces of the same and nail the ¼-in. strips outside the gunwales to protect the canvas there and finish it.

Mix up the paint, give the outside of the canoe two or three coats and while it is drying we will make the paddles and a couple of cushions to sit and kneel in the bottom of the canoe on. Half a gunny sack filled with excelsior or grass makes a good enough cushion and comes in handy for a pillow in camp. Two single paddles 4 ft. long can be joined with a long metal ferrule when a double blade is wanted.

My canoe of this pattern weighs 37 lbs. and is easily portaged by one person or carried about in a light wagon. If punctured by sharp rocks or snags, a piece of canvas and needle and thread will repair the damage, smearing the patch with paint, pitch or grease to make it water tight. I have paddled for miles with a handkerchief poked in a hole in the bot-

tom. By making the canoe a few feet longer, its
capacity will be much greater and of course heavier
material may be used, but the lightness so necessary to
the hunter would be sacrificed. Have used my canoe
safely with three persons in it, total weight about
400 pounds.

Since the above was originally published in H-
T-T. for February, 1904, I have built a slightly
heavier but much stiffer canoe.

This is accomplished by working in two longi-
tudinal strips on each side between the gunwale and
keel board. After the keel board has the bow and
stern posts attached I cut out two moulds, from
rough board. These should be the desired shape of
a cross section of the canoe at about thirty inches from
each end.

The moulds are fastened temporarily to the keel
board and the gunwales and other strips are tacked
to them when they are bent into place. The ribs are
bent outside and fastened to these strips the same as
they are to the gunwales. When most of the ribs
and thwart pieces are fastened in place the moulds
may be knocked out. The length of the ribs is in
this way divided into three spaces and when well
nailed where they cross each strip the canoe is made
much more durable.

But little weight is added as the strips need not
be larger than seven-eighths of an inch square or one-
half by one inch and of some light wood.

The durability of this craft is also increased by
using a heavier weight of canvas—say ten or twelve
ounces to the yard.

A Marsh Skiff.

A skiff of the sort commonly used on the Poto-

mac and Anacostia rivers may be built in three or
four days by any handy boy or man, at an expense
for material of ten dollars or less.

Such a skiff is paddled like a canoe, but is more
easily constructed and less liable to damage than a

A Skiff Traveler's Bank Camp.

canvas craft. I will tell how to make one which
will carry two men or three smaller persons with
safety. It is of shallow draught and narrow beam,
well adapted to small streams and marshes.

The tools necessary to its construction are a
hammer, saw, plane, draw-knife, a brace and bit, or
gimlet, and a screw-driver.

The material may be had wherever there is a
lumber-yard or sawmill and hardware store. Its cost
will vary somewhat with locality, and such changes
as may seem expedient may be made in respect of

the lumber; but the following "bill of material" will suffice:

5 white pine or cypress, planed boards, ⅞ in. thick, 1 ft. wide, 16 ft. long.

3 common siding boards about ½ in. thick, 7 in. wide, 14 ft. long.

1 piece planed plank, 1⅜ in. thick, 6 in. wide and 8 ft. long.

2 lbs. 8 penny, steel, cut nails.

80 1½-in. wood screws.

1 lb. white lead.

1 lb. putty.

½ lb. oakum.

1 can ready-mixed paint.

The sixteen-foot boards should be free from cracks and large or loose knots, as four of them form the outside of the skiff. If thinner boards be used your skiff will be lighter, but must then be stiffened by more crosspieces and knees.

The paint should not be dispensed with, for beside improving the boat's appearance, it fills small cracks and prevents decay. The first work is to cut from the piece of plank two lengths of eighteen inches each, for the bow and stern posts.

Then select two of the sixteen-foot boards for the sides. Cut them square at the ends and of the same length. Make a mark on the side of one board nine inches from the end, and draw a line from the mark to the corner above. Then saw the board off at this angle.

Draw another line two and three-fourths inches from and parallel to the edge you have cut. Next bring the end of the board to a wedge shape by sawing a bevel from this new line to the edge on the opposite side.

Mark and cut the other ends of the side boards in a similar way always remembering which side is intended for the inside and which edge for the bottom. The inside face is of course the face shortened by the bevel cut at each end, and the bottom is that edge of the plank which is eighteen inches shorter than the other edge or top.

After boring eight holes in the ends of the side planks with a bit or gimlet the size of your screws, you can easily fasten the bow and stern posts to one side and one end of the other side.

Before the oblique cuts on the ends of the boards are screwed to the posts, the cuts should be smeared with white lead and the screws smeared, too.

Now cut from the remainder of your plank two strips, two inches wide and thirteen and one-half long; two more sixteen inches long, and a third pair twenty-three inches long.

These strips are to be put across the bottom of the skiff to hold the sides apart and fasten the bottom boards to.

To make the strips fit in nicely, the ends should be cut at such an angle that one side will be an inch shorter than the other. The bottom of the crosspiece should also be a trifle shorter than the top.

The sides of the skiff are now standing in V shape, but with the help of another person or a strap and buckle they can be drawn together at the other end and held until the screws are screwed in. While drawing the ends together, brace the bottom of the sides apart with the short strips of plank so placed as to divide the bottom of the skiff into seven spaces. These strips need not be fastened yet, because the pressure of the sides will probably hold them in place.

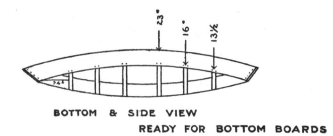

BOTTOM & SIDE VIEW

READY FOR BOTTOM BOARDS

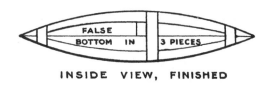

INSIDE VIEW, FINISHED

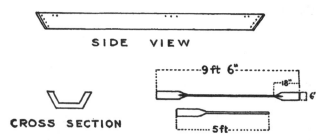

SIDE   VIEW

CROSS SECTION

Cut the bow and stern posts off close to the lower edge of the side boards, which must be planed perfectly flat in order that the bottom boards may fit closely.

After this the crosspieces may be fastened with

two screws at each end, taking care that each piece is perfectly flush with the side boards.

The shortest pair of crosspieces are to be put two feet from the ends, and the others the same distance apart, which should leave the bottom two feet wide in the middle, outside measurement.

If the inner edge of the bottom boards are planed so that when placed together the joint is open like a V, it will hold the caulking much tighter.

By laying these boards on the bottom and marking around with a pencil they may be trimmed off after the bottom has been fastened on.

When the lower edges of the sides have been smeared with white lead and a number of screw-holes made in each bottom board, these may be fastened on. Each bottom board should be screwed to every crosspiece near the joint in the middle of the bottom.

Distribute the remaining screws around the outer edges of the bottom, and complete the work with nails so that the bottom shall be fastened to the sides every three inches.

The edges of the bottom boards are now readily trimmed down with plane and drawing-knife.

With the pieces of board left from the bottom the seats may be made. A triangular seat is put in each end of the skiff, and one about a foot forward of the middle.

The 'ends of the seats should rest on small cleats securely nailed three inches below the upper edge of the sides. The thin boards are for a false bottom, to lie loose on the crosspieces and keep the paddler's feet out of any water which may leak or slop in. This false bottom prevents the bottom from being strained by walking on it. The false bottom is usually made in three pieces for convenience in taking out.

Down the Tennessee in a Mountain Skiff.

Out of the remaining pine board the paddles are made. A double paddle is nine and one-half feet long and a single one five feet. Both have blades eighteen inches long and six inches wide at the end. The paddle-handles may be nicely rounded and the blades made thin and light with the plane and draw-knife.

Now with an old knife or chisel crowd the V-shaped seam in the bottom nearly full of oakum or cotton waste, and cover it with putty.

Cover the nail and screw heads, go over all the seams on the inside and fill any small cracks you may find with the remainder of the putty.

Skiff and paddles may now be painted. Two good coats should be put on.

When used by only one person the paddler generally sits on the middle seat and plies the double paddle.

With two persons the skiff turns best when the second person is in the end seat in the longest division of the boat. Then the single paddles, used on opposite sides, produce the best speed.

The skiff may be paddled either end first, as both are alike. After some practice one person can easily propel the skiff with a single paddle.

These skiffs are used on the tidal marshes in rail-shooting, when they are pushed with a long pole forked at the end to prevent its sinking into the mud. The pusher and the gunner stand, and to a novice their position looks very ticklish. But such skiffs are, however, quite seaworthy.

Trapper's Boat.

I have read so many requests for a trapper's boat, I will send a model I have used and have been making for ten years and will say I never saw their equal.

The first one I made was 14 feet long, 37 inches wide, weight 70 pounds all made of ½-inch pine. This in a pinch will carry four men but will carry two with all their traps, camping outfit, and do it safely. I have used this boat on many a hard trapping trip and had hundreds of dollars worth of fur in it. I had three otters at one time. Now the boat is almost as good as new. I paint it every year, also varnish it with spar varnish. I have a smaller one I made. It is 10 feet long, 33 inches wide and weighs less than 40 pounds. This is fine for one alone but will carry two if they sit near the bottom. I would advise the 14 foot size for general use.

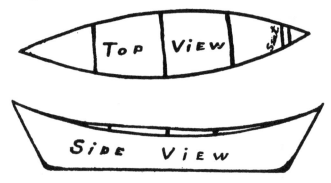

Get two pine or white wood boards 14 feet long, 14 inches wide, ½ inch thick. Lay one board on the other. Saw each end slanting back six inches as per cut. This makes the bottom of the boat one foot shorter than the top. Now bevel the end of each board inside so when spread they will fit smooth. Fasten each end of the boards together loosely with clamp. Spread boards apart so bottom will be 33 and top 37 inches. This spreading will throw bottom of boat down. This should be sawed out so bottom will be straight. Saw each side from end to end and each strip will look like this ◡. Nail ends together with slim wire nails and clinch in the soft wood, or use screws if you like. I use long, slim wire nails now and find them just as good. Put three thwarts of strong wood about the size of a hay fork handle across boat as per cut, about one inch from top of boat. This makes a stiff boat; also handy to lift it with. Only one is needed in a 10 foot boat. Put a one inch ½ round strip on each side of boat the whole length close to edge. Use small wire nails for this about 4 inches apart then clinch them. These strips go on outside of boat. They make a nice finish; also handy when you take hold of sides to pull it over logs or bogs, as you will have to if you trap in big swamps as I do. Take a 1 inch piece, shave it on both sides to an edge to fit in each end. Nail clear through these pieces from side to side, first on one side then the other, then clinch down close, I use about twenty nails to each end. This nailing makes a boat very stiff and strong. True up outsides of each end of boat, then put on half round bang irons. Let them run from top down to and six inches on the bottom. Make one seat in end as per cut for paddler.

For other seats I make folding ones, six inches high, with back or without, as you like. These you can take out. It makes it lighter.

When you carry boat, turn it over with middle thwart across shoulders with hand holds of sides. When alone put stones or some weight in bow. It will then paddle fine. Be sure and saw enough off sides so bottom of boat will be straight. Work slow, take pains. Don't leave boat out all day in the hot sun or in the water to soak day and night. When through for the day pull out and turn over just like you would a canoe.

I built a boat after this pattern in Northern Maine of one inch pine 18 feet long, 4 feet wide. It would carry about 1500 pounds. It cost only $1.85. I made another one in Florida 19 feet long 4 feet wide. This only cost $2.15. I used it in Florida waters for one winter's trapping, paddled it hundreds of miles and it worked fine. I had a big load of traps and camp outfit with two months' provisions so had to have a big boat, but it goes just as smooth and slick as the smaller ones. To make a nice model the sides should not be less than 14 inches wide. This when finished will be 14 inches deep at ends and 10 in the middle. If you want a strong, heavy boat, make it of inch boards. Give it two coats of paint and then one of spar varnish. The paddler's seat should be one inch down inside of boat so cushion won't slip off if you use one.

Don't try to make this boat in a day. Do a good job and every time you step in it and wind your fingers around the paddle shaft, it will be a thing of joy and beauty as well as utility. This boat made of ½ inch pine will weigh about 70 pounds.

Hunter's Boat.

I will give my method of building a boat. It may not be the best but it will answer the purpose. First secure two boards, twelve feet is good length, fourteen inches wide, white pine is best if you can get clear stuff. Then a piece of oak or any hard wood for the nose piece, six or eight inches wide by five inches. Hew in shape of letter V. Have back sides five inches. Then about half way cut from back ⅞ of an inch so the side boards will sink in just even. Then cut two boards as wide as you want your boat. Cut them on a slant so as to give the boat the right shear. The more the boat sides flare, the more shear. Give the boat a good shear to insure easy running and steadiness.

Put in the boards, one a little more than one-third from the front, the other half from that to the back end. Nail to nose piece, then draw back and nail back end. For bottom use inch boards matched, six inches wide, nail on crosswise or put in some ribs and put a bottom on of twenty gauge sheet steel. Nail very closely, that would make it lighter.

I have a steel duck boat with bow facing oars that I think is all right for trapping, hunting and fishing, as it is light, clean and comfortable and runs very easy. No man would use any other than bow facing oars after one trial. I have a small steel pike with a seven foot handle one inch in diameter which is the handiest thing a boat can carry.

Canvas Canoe.

A canoe can be made in the following way: take good hogshead hoops, select the best one and then take two strips of board and fasten them to the keel hoop which has been opened out to form a backbone, bow and stern to keep it upright. Get about 30 good barrel hoops, tying them all along with stout tarred twine to the keel hoop. Two more hogshead hoops are secured, to which is tied one end of each to an end of the keel hoop, bringing the other ends round, tie them to the other end of the keel. This makes the side or rail. The ends or tips of the barrel hoops are next tied to these rail hoops. This produces a skeleton complete.

To get a good pattern, paste some old newspapers together and lay them on the skeleton. Now cut some heavy twilled bed ticking to fit and have it sewed together. This cover is put on and over the frame and painted with boiled linseed oil and burnt umber. It can also be waterproofed by taking six ounces of hard yellow soap and one-half pint of water, add one-half pound patent dryer and five pounds boiled linseed oil, applying with a brush.

Another Canvas Boat.

In answer to a trapper in Morrison Co., Minn., in regard to making a light canvas canoe, inclosed you will find drawing of one that I made.

Two side pieces AA should be made of green oak one-half inch thick and two inches wide. They should be fastened at end with screws, BB and spread by braces CCC, as shown in the cut. For a twelve-foot canoe, I spread these strips forty inches in the center.

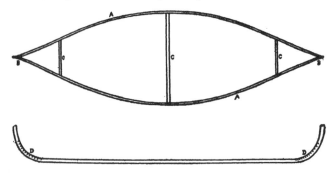

I make the bottom piece of one and one-half inch green oak. To bend it, make saw cuts as shown in drawing DD. These saw cuts should be three-fourths inch apart, for a distance of nine inches. The strip must be well soaked so that it will bend easily.

The ribs of this boat are made of green oak $\frac{1}{4}$ inch thick, $1\frac{1}{2}$ inches wide and can be had at any saw-mill for 25 cents. In putting ribs on the boat, I use lathing nails. The wire nails are best, 6 nails to a rib, 2 in center on bottom, 2 at each end of rib on top and those on top will drive through and clinch. Place ribs about $2\frac{1}{2}$ inches apart on frame through the widest part of the boat. I make the rib reach from the top piece on one side, around bottom to the top piece on the opposite side; do this until you get near the ends, then you can use short pieces to reach from bottom to top and tack these short ribs to side of bottom. This gives the boat a nice shape at each end. After I get my ribs all on, I take a strip of the same stuff ribs are made of and run from end to end on the inside of frame and tack this piece to each one. It is best to put two of these pieces on, as it makes the ribs stiffer. Now your frame with ribs on is supposed to be soaked in water when you started to frame it; let it dry out a couple of days, then paint frame good, inside and out. Now you are ready for canvas.

Canvas need not be wide enough to reach entirely around the boat. You can get narrow canvas that will reach around from bottom to top; lap over on bottom, place tacks three-fourths inch apart in canvas on bottom, then nail strip over this lap at bottom, after you have painted canvas, also at top on inside gunwale.

The boat that I made cost $3.50 complete, was 11 feet long and would carry two men easily but was tricky on account of round bottom. They are very easy to get used to and ride the water like a duck, are light, easy to handle, and give good service. On a lake they will last three years, if it has a muddy shore and no stones to snag.

It is best to build a platform of $\frac{1}{2}$ inch light boards for bottom; this also protects the canvas and ribs in bottom. Do not take piece out of center that was put in to spread frame, or piece across the top from end to end, until the frame is dried out; then the boat will hold its shape. The small braces in end of boat I leave in and cover over with canvas board up from bottom. They make nice little lockers for storing traps and fishing tackle.

A Canvas Canoe.

To those who wish to make a servicable canvas canoe for hunting and trapping purposes, I submit the following method, having made ten of these canoes and found them satisfactory.

I make the long strips to go next to the canvas, one-half or one-third inch thick and for the ribs I use barrel hoops, placed one and one-half inches apart.

The canvas should be shaped as shown in the cut and the part marked AA is first nailed securely to the bow and the other end fastened in a similar manner to the stern.

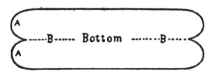

When the canvas has been fastened all around, a strip of wood one inch wide and as long as the canoe is fastened on the bottom at BB; then paint with hot tar along the sides of this strip and on the ends of the canoe.

The canoe must be made fairly wide or it will

tip over easily. The width for a ten-foot canoe should be two feet three inches and the depth ten inches. Canvas must be well stretched over frame.

Boat Building.

I send you a plan of a boat. I have made a number of them and like them very well for general use along streams. I use 16-foot lumber for the sides 14 inches wide and then I have enough off of the ends for the end seat and locker. If you want to you can use 14-foot lumber and get an extra board for the locker and seats. For the bottom, I use 14-foot lumber 16 inches wide. The sides and bottom I make out of good first-class white pine five-eights of an inch thick.

No. 1 is side view of boat inside. I put seats down pretty low, but some will prefer them higher. A boat doesn't tip so easily when seats are down low. I also put a six-inch board to step on, instead of stepping on the bottom. One is liable to jump in sometimes in a hurry, so the board saves the bottom in that way. By jumping on the board instead of the bottom, one doesn't spring the bottom boards any. I put in a locker in each end of the boat, but if one chooses to leave them out, he can do so. One I fix so it can be used for a seat and it is made so one can put a lock on. I do this so that I can lock up things which I don't want to take along if I happen to want to leave the boat for awhile.

Now, as to the making of the boat. I cut the bow and stern pieces out the shape of No. 3 which I make out of 3 x 6 oak and about 18 or 20 inches long; then I plane them smooth after they are sawed out.

No. 4 is the shape of side when cut out. I cut out strip on bottom side of board which leaves the bot-

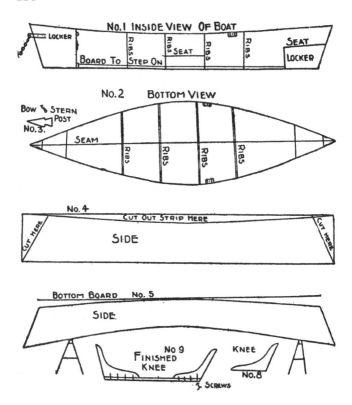

No. 1 INSIDE VIEW OF BOAT

LOCKER | RIBS | RIBS | SEAT | RIBS | RIBS | SEAT
BOARD TO STEP ON | LOCKER

No. 2　　BOTTOM VIEW

BOW & STERN POST
No. 3.
SEAM | RIBS | RIBS | RIBS | RIBS

No. 4
CUT OUT STRIP HERE
CUT HERE | SIDE | CUT HERE

BOTTOM BOARD　　No. 5
SIDE.
No 9 FINISHED KNEE　　KNEE
No. 8
SCREWS

tom more straight, but can be left on if one chooses to.

Now, as to the knees. I make them out of oak, natural crook and they are easily made. I go to the woods and find a tree that has a limb on about four inches thick of the proper angle for the knee. Cut the tree down and cut a notch half through about a foot and a half below the limb and one the same close to limb on upper side. Then split out like No. 6 and then split in halves again and that makes the two for one set of knees.

No. 7 shows the knee split out in the rough.

No. 8 shows the knee finished.

No. 9 shows the knees put together and ready to

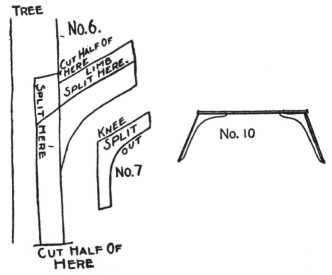

fasten sides to like No. 10. I leave top part of knees long enough to come to top of sides, which makes it that much stronger. I use four pair of knees and the seat and locker does for the ends instead of putting in more knees.

When I put in the two middle sets of knees, I take a rope with a loop on one end to put on the end of the sides; then draw the ends close together. Take the bow and stern posts, put on a thick coating of white lead where the sides fit in. Put post in place and fasten with clamps tightly and then bore one-fourth inch holes through sides and stern post and put in rivets and rivet them solid. If the sides don't bend very easy I take a pail of hot water and a cloth and wet the outside of the sides and that will help quite a bit. When I get the stern and bow posts in I put in the other two sets of knees. Then I turn the bottom side of the boat up, as No. 5, dress edges of the bottom boards and lay them on the boat. Drive a nail down into the posts through the bottom board to hold them in place. Take a pencil and mark around the edges of the sides on the bottom and trim off the bottom boards to the pencil mark and the bottom is ready to nail on as in No. 5. Use screws or wrought nails for fastening. I like screws best for one doesn't have to pound any as in using clinch nails.

The bottom is nailed on to the sides instead of nailing the sides to the bottom like some boats are made. When the bottom is nailed on, I calk the seams with cotton batting. Very likely some of the boys will say that it is no good, but I have never had to calk a boat twice with it. When I get it calked, I thin down some white lead so it will be about as thin as a thick syrup and pour on the seam and when it dries, turn the boat over and do the other side the same. When it gets thoroughly dry, I give the boat two coats of good paint, put in oar lock sockets and put on the finishing touches and when the paint is dry, the boat is ready to use.

If such a boat is taken care of, it will last a long time, and it need not cost a great deal. I have to pay from $70 to $80 a thousand for lumber here to build a good boat but very likely lumber can be bought for less in many places.

A River Skiff — Good Traveling Model.

BICYCLE OR MOTORCYCLE TENDER.

The cabin-boat is simply a movable house, which one tows or floats or poles from place to place, down stream or around a lake. There are cabin-boaters who have tents up the bank and shacks and even extra cabin-boats in which to store outfits and dogs, etc.

Anything that increases the efficiency of the cabin-boat is worth considering, and in this matter one often meets the difficulty of transportation over land. It is easy enough to go in a canoe or row-boat but always there has been the feeling that one could not see enough of the land, or go far enough afield. People say of boating that it is too confining—that all one has is the creek or river or lake.

"Now if one could only have a horse, he'd be all right on the river", I had a cabin-boater say to me, speaking of the difficulties of peddling from a cabin-boat.

The bicycle of a few years ago, and now the motorcycle and soon the cycle-car, are having a tremendous influence on all out-door branches. The motorcycle will take one anywhere that there is a space wide enough to run two wheels over. It will climb mountains, romp through mud, and go twenty or thirty miles in an hour.

Of course, one must be quite expert to ride mud, but it is done. One of my friends came out of the woods over a rough road through snow and mud. Some men ride all winter, in spite of snow. The development of good roads in some states is going to make marvelous changes in out-door life of all kinds, and the cabin-boater is already feeling the change. A cabin-boater with a motorcycle on boat has only to tie up at a ferry, and he can ride out fifty miles and back, the same day; this, almost regardless of the condition of the road, if it is not too thick with clay.

Here, then, is an entirely new opening for the trapper. He can trap a creek forty miles away, in the next county, in the next state, and live at home. This means the opening up of great areas of country where trapping is too poor to tempt one to go there for a campaign, yet inviting enough for a day's trapping a week. The little muskrat marsh, twenty miles away, worthy of some attention, will get it from the motor-cycler or bicycler.

Earlier in the season, the hunters will find their hunting field practically unlimited. A man can start on his motorcycle, ride a hundred miles, shoot a mess of birds or rabbits, and return, all within twenty-four hours. If one lives within a hundred miles of a game country, the motorcycle puts it within reach, providing the roads are adequate.

This means that the man who lives in a house-boat can hunt in the mountains, and not stay away from home more than a night or two, if as much. We all know that there is game in scattered woodlots, in scattered fields. The time and effort that is wasted getting from one hunting place to another is what kills the days' hunting and success. What takes half an hour to walk is covered in three minutes or less on the motorcycle following the roads.

The motorcycle and bicycle are almost as much a necessity on a cabin-boat as the skiff.

Where there is any gasolene on board, be sure and have something where it can be reached to throw on the gasoline in case it catches fire. Sand in boxes, and an extinguisher or two are life-savers.

CHAPTER IX.

The Gasoline Launch.

UNQUESTIONABLY, a gasoline launch will add greatly to the pleasure of cabin boating. A little motor in the stern of an ordinary skiff will do wonders in the way of managing a cabin-boat, making landings and keeping off the bank in a wind. But taking care of the motor requires tact, patience and considerable skill. The more skill as a mechanic one has the more successful will be the attempts to start a motor and keep it going.

One should understand the engine so well that it can be taken all apart and assembled. It takes experience to run some kinds of machines well—and these are frequently the best ones to have, being steadier, more reliable, and in the long run, more satisfactory.

The hull of the launch should be substantial, and if one is going to a rainy section, like the Mississippi bottoms, it is a good thing, even a necessary thing, to have the boat covered with some kind of a water shed, lest it fill in a night. Of course, waves may swamp a launch of small size, and wind may turn it over. A swamped launch is likely to be a lost launch, for most of them sink because of the weight of the engine. Water-tight compartments will avoid this, and may save lives.

If the engine, or dynamo, or battery get wet, there is sure to be trouble. This can be avoided to some extent by having tarpaulin to put over the apparatus at night, or in storms. But the gasoline launcher

is always between two difficulties. If he closes his
engine up in a cabin, there may be a leak, which will
lead to an explosion. If it is in the open, there may
be a storm that will fill the engine pit with waves or
rain.

It is hoped and believed that alcohol engines will
soon be in use, which will do away with the necessity
of using the more dangerous gasoline. Doubtless, the
alcohol launch will reduce the motorman's troubles to
a considerable extent. The kerosene motors and
burners of distillate are now developed to a point of
very high efficiency.

So long as the motor runs along all right there
is nothing to do but keep the feed, the wires, and
sundry fixings in proper condition. But sooner or
later a hitch comes. Something begins to pound,
something puffs smoke, something fails to act. Then
it requires ingenuity to locate the difficulty and to
make a repair when located.

The main thing is patience; the next, observation,
and last of all, skill. "Don't do too much" can be
said oftener to a man fixing a gasoline motor than
any other phrase. Such a little thing out of whack
will make all the trouble at times. Perhaps a little
spring is too tense, or too weak. A bit of brass wire,
coiled and put in place of the old one is all that is
needed at the most. Sometimes a mere stretching
of the spring will serve.

The man on a cruise will have a dynamo, as well
as a set or two of storage batteries. The battery will
store up the surplus electricity against future use.
Sometimes when bucking the wind and all the power
is needed, the dynamo belt is jumped off, and the
sparks taken from the battery, to save power. The
battery will also light the cabin-boat cabin with elec-

Erie Canal Boat and Launch.

tricity for an hour or so—even all night if desired.
But all these little things must be looked out for and
taken care of. In case of necessity one should be
able to use the motor engine to saw wood for the
stove, or haul in the handy line, or do any one of a
thousand things for which power is required. It is
not merely a boat engine, but an engine for other
service as well.

It is worth while having a good set of machine
tools with one if he is engineering a motor. With
these tools almost any repairs can be made to a broken
engine. I've seen a motor that had been broken at the
top of one cylinder. The crank inside got loose and
punched off the top. The fisherman took a file and
smoothed the rough broken edge. He bored holes
into the top of the cylinder and threaded them. He
took a plate of iron and bored holes around the edge
to fit the holes in the cylinder, put in some wagon
bolts, started up his engine and went to a repair shop
to have the cylinder fixed. The mechanic looked at
it and said, "What more do you want? I can't improve that, except its looks, perhaps."

You can sometimes fix an engine with an ax
and a monkey wrench, but certain tools are good to
have along. These are:

A set of taps and dies, machine set, up to half
an inch.

Good monkey wrench—ninety cents, or so.
Six-inch wrench.
Two or three drop forge steel S wrenches.
Pair of ten-inch pipe wrenches.
Pair of gas pliers, eight-inch.
Pair Cronk button pliers.
Large and small screw drivers (two).
Light machine hammer.

Hack saw, and dozen hack saw blades.

A few assorted files—rattail, three-cornered, round and flat files, at least.

Squirt oil can, small size.

Half-inch cold chisel and cape chisel.

Emery cloth, fine.

Soldering iron.

Odds and ends of pipes, Ls and street Ls, brass connections, nipples, copper wire, brass wire, ball of wicking, sheet of asbestos for packing, wire for electric apparatus, litmus paper to test poles (negative pole makes blue mark on wet litmus), Babbitt metal for bearings, etc., etc.

Callipers, small rule, square, etc.

For woodwork likely to be necessary, one has in the cabin-boat outfit an ax, a saw, plane, claw hammer, brace and bits, including an extension bit with extra blades, one-half inch chisel. The ax can be made to serve as a hatchet, but seventy-five cents invested in a good hatchet is worth the money.

These tools will pay for themselves. With them about everything can be done that can be done outside a machine shop. If one adds a little vise to his outfit, time will be saved in making bolts, nuts, fittings or what not. Scrutiny of the engine always repays the little time it takes. A little tightening, a new packing, some fresh oil—best quality for gas chamber —an occasional overhauling on a rainy day, will more than repay. It will be adding compound interest to an investment that might otherwise be lost, or greatly depreciated in value.

If anything goes to smash, having learned what is the matter, let plenty of time be taken in considering what had best be done. If a storm is coming up, it will be better to work the sweeps and get into shelter before doing anything at all. If the bolts in the cylinder head have blown off, perhaps some one sitting on the end of a beam holding down the head may enable one to make a landing across wide water; but on the whole, it's better to make a chute, or safe enough landing, eat something, take a smoke and perhaps wait until next day before monkeying with a bad job. In the meanwhile, it is pretty sure to be ascertained that this world is not all a wilderness of woe.

If a connecting rod break, a new one can sometimes be made of material at hand, but sometimes it's easier just to cut screw threads on the broken ends, cut threads to match in a bit of brass pipe, and then screw them together with the gas pliers or pipe wrench.

Watch should be kept on the propeller, lest it work loose. A key put through the hole in the end of the shaft will keep the propeller from slipping off and sinking, in case it works loose. A good reversible propeller simplifies launch traveling and is especially valuable when towing a cabin-boat.

The gasoline tank is usually under the bow deck of a launch, where it balances, to some extent, the weight of the engine. A pipe lead to the engine ought to come down the outside of the boat, so that a leak will not fill the cabin with explosive fumes.

If one has to disconnect the pipes when the joints are replaced, the threads should be coated with shellac. Failure to do this is likely to waste gasoline, and perhaps indirectly destroy the boat, through an explosion.

Practically all the accidents to gasoline launches are due solely to carelessness. Trouble will come, of course, but the man habitually careful with his gasoline boat, his cabin-boat and fire arms can sometimes take long chances with them that another who has weakened them, could not think of taking.

Gasoline motorboats are now so plenty that very inexpensive ones may be had. For ordinary cabin-boat towing, four to six horsepower in a stout launch will take the large boat anywhere desired. There are many house-boats being built which have motors to drive them, instead of using oars. A small stern wheel, and a six horsepower motor would drive a thirty-foot house-boat as fast as needed, but this is not a matter quite inside the limits of this little hand-book. It is worth considering, however. They are not difficult to install, and all the motor engine manu-facturers are glad to give advice on this technical subject.

CHAPTER X.

What to Wear.

THERE is no reason why life on a cabin-boat should be lived in rags and tatters. They do not lead to comfort. One can carry as good clothes for river-town experience as is desired. Ordinarily the best is kept in a trunk, while working clothes are worn while afloat.

For ordinary wear, first of all, let the cloth be substantial, and of wool. Corduroy, cottons and other clammy garments, should be avoided outside or next to the skin. Light woolen underwear and medium-weight suits are best. Such sweaters, socks and negligee shirts as the wearer most enjoys should be worn. A coat at the sweeps or shooting is much less comfortable than a sweater. A game bag is less shoulder binding than a heavy coat. But as to this, the experienced hunter knows what he wants, if he knows what to expect.

On the Mississippi it will be damp, very chilly at times and simply glorious at others. It will be outdoors living to a large extent. There is shooting from sand bar blinds in howling, sleet-laden gales, and in warm rains; woods roaming, and always a call for medium-weight shoes, or rubber boots, and rarely need of so-called hunting leathers, or moccasins, etc. Hip boots for wet weather walking or hunting and a mackintosh or rubber coat, or oilskins serve to keep one dry, but the hardier spirit takes the rain on his sweater and changes his clothes on returning to the boat. One does not often catch cold on a cabin-boat, though he

A View at Arkansas City Landing.

should not trust to this rule too much. Woolens and a warm boat go far toward keeping one comfortable at all times.

A woman will find short skirts best for the ordinary life in a cabin-boat and at the usual landings. Moderately heavy shoes and a pair of high boots will permit her to share the pleasures of the outing at all times. For going over the levees "up town" the latest fashions will not be too new, if she is to meet friends. But with her, as with her husband, she should consider whether it is worth while to carry the best when ordinary street wear, or even morning garb will serve every purpose.

In fitting out for a cabin-boat trip down the Mississippi or its tributaries, it should not be forgotten that one will find more kinds of mud, and more kinds of wet weather than most mortals have ever experienced. if one is prepared for pleasant weather, cold and warm rains, and soft ground, one has enough.

Reasonable, not freak, hats should be worn. Headgear that the wind cannot snatch off is a necessity. An old soft Fedora felt hat, with the lining torn out, is excellent. Broad-brimmed hats are often worn by cabin-boaters because they shelter the eyes and face from sun and pelting rain.

It is desirable to have rain-proofed garments and ponchos—capes. An effective waterproofing is made by boiling the shirt or garment in very soapy water— three cakes of soap to six quarts of water. Then dip the garment in a pail of water in which a pound of alum has been dissolved. This process shrinks the garments somewhat, but an extra large blouse made out of dyed duck, say, and treated in this way will shed water in the hardest rain storm. Two or three treatments insure every opening being filled with the soap, which is made insoluble by the alum. An old coat in good condition and large enough to bear a little shrinking is well waterproofed by this process. So are tents, capes, etc. A pair of overalls, a jacket and a hat so treated make an excellent storm protection.

How to Keep Warm in Rubber Boots.

An H-T-T writer says:

When I buy rubber boots, I get them large enough to permit me to wear three pairs of socks and a pair of fleece-lined moccasins. The first pair of socks are cotton, then over them two pairs of woolen socks, then put on your fleece-lined cotton moccasins and draw on your rubber boots. The boots should fit snug but not tight. If you do this, no matter how cold it gets you can wade in ice water for hours and your feet will remain warm.

This combination is far ahead of felt boots for several reasons. First they are much lighter and warmer than felt. Second, they can be taken apart and dried by a fire in a few minutes if you happen to get over your boot tops in water. Third, you can wade water much deeper than you can with felt boots and rubber shoes. Try this, brother trapper, and you will never buy another pair of felt boots.

I use the "Ball Brand" rubber boots because they are neater and have tops two inches higher than the top on any other brand I know of, but don't buy roll shoes, they carry more mud and don't wear any longer. These are facts learned by experience.

Another thing, when you purchase your rubber boots, tell your dealer to give you a pair that has not laid over from last year, because rubber boots that have been carried over in the retail store are liable to go to pieces sooner than those fresh from the jobber, for light damages rubber. Some men will buy a pair of rubber boots that have been carried over and exposed to light and air and then blame the factory for turning out bad goods. All rubber goods rot very quickly if exposed to light and air. The factories and wholesale dealers have a way of preserving them and keeping them good in heavy brown paper and putting them in a cool, dark place helps to keep them.

Don't forget that this information is not theoretical. I have learned it by experience. Another thing, when you go trapping, wear a good leather belt around your waist over your coat. Carry your hatchet stuck in it, with the edge turned toward the back, wear it on your left side well around toward your hip pocket and you don't know how handy it is.

CHAPTER XI.

THINGS TO EAT.

THE cabin-boater will find it to his advantage to live as the natives live. Above Cairo there are vast quantities of fruit, and one can lay in supplies of preserves, fruit butters, etc. Here, too, one will find vegetables at the small landings for sale at their cheapest. This applies to points below St. Louis particularly. The market reports of St. Louis papers will give one an idea of what is to be had to eat in Missouri and Illinois.

Below Cairo, one misses the fruits, until the lower river is reached, where tropical fruits are found. The traveler will do well to watch the localities and pick out the things he most enjoys at each place.

In Missouri, say, one finds sorghum, or china sugar cane molasses. It is most delicious, and eaten with biscuit and good butter stands a typical dish of the region from Ozark mountains through Kentucky and Tennessee well up to Pennsylvania. The butter is stirred cold into the molasses and the hot biscuit sopped in it.

One will do well to linger between St. Louis and Cairo, or down the Ohio or upper Tennessee because of the delicacies to be found there.

Of course, foodstuffs, the sweet potatoes, tomatoes, corn, etc., are at their best. At every town, and between most towns, one will find fish markets, or fishermen from whom fish may be purchased. Of course, one can catch enough fish for his own use, almost anywhere, if he is willing to take the trouble to learn how. As a general rule, the fish buyer will do well to get only river fish; the lake fish are softer and less savory. Fish from a very deep lake—say 75 feet or more—are not affected by the summer heat, however, and are good. Carp and catfish are the coarser kinds, and "game fish" consist of black bass and "trout" or perch. Bass are sometimes called trout. The game fish are found in the lakes and one should go prepared for them as to fishing tackle. For fishing hints, a separate chapter has been prepared.

Game is abundant in many places. There should be no trouble in keeping ducks, coons, 'possums, squirrels, etc., etc., in the meat hanger or cooler. The northerner will do well to consider the merits of four-and-twenty black birds baked in a pie. Of hunting and trapping one's own fresh meat, more will be told.

One should not forget the nutritive and comforting value of hickory, pecan and other nuts, large as hen eggs, found below Cairo at various landings. These constitute a regular article of diet. Pecans are also to be had by the ton, for the gathering. The nut landings should be sought out from the start up and down. Corona, Tenn., is a hickory-nut landing, Paine's Landing, Ark., is notable for pecans.

Wild honey, wild grapes, soft-shell turtles, snapping turtles and land terrapin, the breasts of blue herons, fat gulls, venison, bear meat, etc., etc., are among the local dishes to be had. The epicure must take care to associate with the cabin-boaters, landing keepers and others, inquiring about things eatable if he would learn the resources of the landings where he stops.

Of course, there are regular articles of diet to be provided. Salt pork, or bacon, flour, beans, potatoes, etc., etc., are carried just as one has them in a station-

A Drifter's Raft.

ary house, but the river diet varies more than a home diet. One will find eggs on the Atchafayala River selling for four dozen for two bits—about six cents a dozen. But chickens are about forty cents each because the darkies buy them.

Biscuit made with soda and sour milk, or baking powder, take the place of potatoes in the East. Hot bread is served at every meal, and one can mix sour milk, soda, salt and flour, cut the dough into biscuit and bake it as quickly as he can peel and cook potatoes. At the cities, one can purchase baker's bread, but the price is high for small loaves. Good "old bread," however is to be had at five cents a loaf.

Beef is often on sale at the landing stores, or commissaries, during the winter. In towns one will find butcher shops a plenty where one can puchase soup bones or good steaks, but the stranger will do well to keep his eye on what he orders, in most places. Purchases are made by "five cents' worth", fifteen cents' worth, etc. Buying by the pound is seldom practiced, in towns or out on most cabin-boat rivers. Sugar, for instance, is put up in ten-cent packages.

One should have a filtering jug for water. Most river men drink the Mississippi mud without a qualm, and the tenderfoot soon becomes a clay-lined cabin-boater. Nevertheless a filter furnishing clear water is a delight. For photograph work, it is a prime necessity.

One can stand poor grub and irregular meals for a week or two, but the man afloat should make up his mind to have his three meals a day, and have them well cooked. There will be emergencies when meals will be delayed and for such times, cakes of sweet chocolate, or canned goods should be provided. A full stomach will change the face of a dismal prospect quicker than anything else on a river. One can have

10 C. B. P.

everything in a cabin-boat that he can in a house on shore. By ordinary diligence and observation, his "fancy" diet should completely change every hundred miles from the apples and wild turkeys of the hills to the oranges, bananas and oysters of Vicksburg and below.

For emergencies everywhere, there should be on hand a supply of the prepared dried foods—erbswurst, lentils, dry soups, hard-tack, canned soups, dried vegetables, etc. In five minutes with these prepared soups one is able to prepare a fit meal for the hungriest of mortals, and if they are kept in their original packages, they last almost indefinitely. They are not expensive to eat, though more expensive, of course, than the things prepared from raw materials.

One who is out doors a good deal of the time needs plenty of sugar, and it is a good idea to have candy or candy recipes for a cabin-boat change of fare, or desert.

CHAPTER XII.

Cabin Boat Expenses.

THE cost of house-boating or cabin-boating depends entirely on the waters frequented, the ones afloat and the time taken for the experience.

"Good livers" at Memphis say that twenty-five cents a day will keep a person in food. This, the tourist will find reasonable for hearty but not fancy eating. A fair hunter and fisherman will easily supply a boat with meats at the expense of ammunition, a few traps and fishing tackle. But time must be taken for hunting—special effort must be made to keep oneself always in meat and fish.

The first cost is getting to the river side, the second purchasing or building the boat, the third getting a skiff, fourth the outfit, and fifth, the daily food.

The boat will cost from $25 up, and a fit one for two or more persons, $50 or more, in all probability. One should look further before paying more than $100 for an ordinary river houseboat, unless it is new, in first-class condition, of good wood, and far up the stream. Some river store boats, nearly 100 feet long and 18 feet wide are worth upwards of $1000. A first-class, 30-foot pine boat, painted and equipped, even furnished, is frequently sold for from $60 to $100, and rarely $150.

One could build a boat at Knoxville, Pittsburg, St. Louis, St. Paul, Shreveport, Memphis, Evansville, etc., etc., live in it a few months, and then sell it at Paducah, Memphis, Helena, Arkansas City or other down the river places. The cost of building, if $100, would be more than half returned, or even all and more returned, providing an anxious customer was found. A cabin-boat can always be sold at nearly half its cost within a year or two. Paint, pretty trimmings, curtains and a neat interior go far toward selling a craft.

A new clinker-built skiff of first-class make, 16 feet long, costs $24.50 at St. Louis. A fisherman's flat-bottomed skiff runs about a dollar a foot up to twenty feet. Second-hand boats vary in price, good ones costing nearly as much as new, unless one catches a seller about to leave the river, when the price is often very low.

Ropes are sold by the pound. One can get them second-hand, but new ones of half the size are usually more reliable. Ropes vary in weight and cost. It will pay the cabin-boater to put $10 or $15 in ropes— mooring lines, and a 500-foot one-half inch handy line.

An anchor will cost from $1.50 up, depending on the size. Frequently second-hand ones can be picked up in junk stores, of which every large river town has one or two.

A wood cook stove, with oven, of cabin-boat size, can be had for $3 to $5. A second-hand one will serve. The stove pipe goes through the roof, and the upper link should be galvanized. A good hood over the top of the pipe is advisable to keep out the rain. An oil stove with at least two covers is a good investment at $1.50 or more. One can do good and ample cooking over an oil stove. A blue flame stove which doesn't have to be perfectly level is better than a common yellow flame apparatus. The best three-hole blue flame costs $11, and a large oven, $2.50

more. A two-hole will serve for roughing it. The oil stoves do very well for heating a tight boat, and a special oil heater is a comfort worth the two or three dollars, and oil it costs.

Wood, of course costs nothing but the trouble of getting and cutting it. One can cook his meals or meals for two or three with less than two gallons of oil a week—say twenty-four cents a week. Heating would cost three times as much, if oil alone were burned. By taking a wood-and-soft-coal heater, and an oil stove for cooking, the boat will be well equipped for from $6 to $12. A wood heater made of sheet iron, and burning "chunks" is an excellent cabin-boat winter stove. The oil stove is best for cooking, winter and summer.

If a bunk is made of boards, filled with straw and covered with old bedding, the cost is little or nothing. A cot, with a thick quilt doubled on the canvas, and covered with two other quilts of cheap though effective quality, need cost little more than $3. An iron bedstead can be put in for $3, a mattress for $5, and appropriate bedding for $4 or $5 more. For a long journey, it is advisable to have muslin sheets, and cither blankets or quilts, or both. All down the Mississippi, one will find women at most steamboat landings glad to do washings. It is hardly worth while to have one's camping equipage ironed.

Granite or enameled ware dishes are more satisfactory than others for cooking and even table service. Of course earthenware dishes for the food can be taken, but it should be cheap stuff, not easily broken.

Furniture of stout make, second hand, is cheapest. Cane and wicker chairs, including an easy chair or two, are worth having for the sake of comfort. A few dollars can be spent to good advantage in fur-

niture. But let the cabin-boaters go afloat first with
the bare necessities. As the real need of things is felt,
get them. In this way a boat becomes appropriately
furnished without setting useless things up the bank.

A hammock is very pleasant in a boat, or between
trees up the bank at landings, in warm weather. Hammocks, with blankets sewed into bag shape, and a
thickness or two of quilt next to the cords or canvas,
make excellent sleeping places. If the cabin-boaters
prefer, they can use strips of heavy canvas for their
beds, rigging from fork, or stringing ropes so as to
make berths or hammocks. The canvas and bedding
is folded up by day and is very economical and light
to carry, saved for a future trip.

Food costs according to quality and remoteness
or scarcity of producers. If one eats what a region
furnishes altogether, expenses will be cut to the bone.
Thus, in the fruit country of Illinois and Missouri
in late summer and fall, much of one's diet could and
should be made of inexpensive or even free fruits.
These, with corn, sweet potatoes, sorghum molasses,
biscuit, sundry vegetables and game comprise ample
diet for any man. If one keeps an account of what
he eats, the cost will come somewhere under twenty
cents a day on the river from St. Louis to Cairo,
everything being purchased of producers; but below
Cairo, one finds that many of the farmers raise cotton
and buy everything they eat from the North and East
—consequently prices grow higher as one goes down
the river.

Always, however, one can catch fish, shoot enough
game, gather enough nuts, and use only local products
to keep costs down. From far up the Holston, Alleghany and Clinch, down to the Mississippi Bottoms,
the voyager will be able to lay in supplies at a nominal

cost, or simply for the fun of gathering. A big expense is unnecessary and is rather to be frowned upon.

Let the cabin-boater journeying down the river lay in supplies where articles are least expensive. Sorghum is to be had at its best on the Mississippi in Missouri and Illinois. Apple butter and other fruit butters should be purchased of the farmer people who make them—and there is none better to be had than that made in the mountains of Tennessee, through which the house-boat rivers flow.

In cold weather, it will pay to buy a little black hog for two or three dollars, or a calf, or beef at a few cents a pound. It may happen that the cabin-boater will strike some Arkansas swamp man who wants wild hogs killed on the shares—shot like game.

There are a thousand economies to be practiced in cabin-boat food supplies, the main one being, buy what "everybody eats" at the various landings. Apple butter and home canned fruits in the mountains and green molasses and bananas along the "coast" of Louisiana.

One can get a single shot .30-30 rifle for $5.50. This will do for any game of large size in the Mississippi bottoms, and is especially good for geese shooting on sand bars. A single barreled shotgun will do good work against most kinds of game—squirrels, ducks, coons, 'possum and the like. A $6 or $8 gun will do—of course a double barreled gun of best make is better—but a single barreled gun at $7 is better than a double barreled gun at $10. The best gauge is always a matter of opinion, but a 12 or 16 gauge, loaded with chilled 4s will kill wild geese and wild turkeys, and 6s will bring fox squirrels from a very high tree. The market shooter of the Mis-

Picture Rocks, Tennessee River — Among the Mountain Ranges.

sissippi uses a pump gun and these shooters kill the ducks by the thousands.

A cabin-boat should have a shotgun or rifle for every one aboard who cares to shoot. The shotgun will be used much oftener than the big game rifle. If there are to be three hunting weapons on a boat, a .30-30, a 22 Winchester repeater and a seven-pound shotgun would be nearly an ideal equipment. Of course, a .38-55 single shot, or a .32-40 repeater would be good. In fact, a long-range rifle, a squirrel rifle and a bird, rather duck, gun, are good equipments for fun, on the Mississippi.

But let it not be forgotten that all the states along the Mississippi have non-resident hunting and trapping laws. They were all made because of market shooters who followed the game flights and slaughtered regardless of native rights. The decent, gentlemanly sportsman is not interfered with. But the man who shoots for market, or hogs the game, is sure to be. Failure to respect local sentiment is likely to add a heavy fine to the expenses of a cabin-boat journey.

One can carry a camera of any size on a cabin-boat. A 5 x 7 costing about $30 is a good boat instrument. But for one who must count the cost it is better to get a $24, or cheaper, 3¼ x 4¼, because the plates cost less than half as much and one takes many more pictures. Under "Photographing" is discussed the camera question to some length.

In order to give a general idea of the cost of a trip, it is worth while to make out a list of things that require an outlay of money. Suppose two persons are going for a trip down the Mississippi from St. Louis to New Orleans. A liberal allowance would be:

Cabin-boat and equipment $100
Food 45
Furnishings 25
Rifle, shotgun, revolver 18
Ammunition 10
Fishing tackle   5
Tools   6
Skiff 25
Oil, paint, nails, extras, etc............. 25
                                        ———
Total $239

This is for a three-months' journey and makes
no allowance for the sale of the boat and furnishings
at the end of that time. If the journey was made
from St. Paul to St. Louis, Cairo or Memphis, doubtless $50 would be received for the boat and its equip-
ment, the skiff, the weapons, furnishings, etc. Thus
the net cost would be brought down to $164, for two
persons—$27.50 a month, say. For six months, the
expense is considerably less per month than this.
With a tar paper boat, no skiff and bone-clean outfit,
the trip might cost less than $100 for three months.

Everything depends on the travelers and their
natural food demands. One could live just as cheap-
ly now as a hundred years ago, except as to certain
staples. By cutting the diet down to cornmeal and
one's own fish and game, the cost would be very low.
On the other hand, prices of fancy stuffs make the
costs mount hand over fist.

CHAPTER XIII.

Cabin-Boating Waters.

ASTONISHING distances can be traveled in the United States by people in cabin-boats. House-boats have been launched up the Yellowstone and brought safely down to New Orleans—from the Rocky Mountains to within 130 miles of the Gulf of Mexico, a journey of more than 3000 miles. One can start up the Allegheny, Tennessee, Cumberland, Illinois, Mississippi, Arkansas, Red, Yazoo, etc., and follow the windings of the stream chosen for hundreds of miles and most of the time in placid, indolent comfort so far as managing the boat is concerned.

Some rivers take more skill than others, of course. If one insisted on having adventures with a spice—not too strong—of danger, such streams as the Holston, Clinch, French Broad or other swift flowing rivers could be chosen. A twenty-foot house-boat, launched, say, at Saltville, Va., could be taken clear to New Orleans, but the trip down the Little Holston must be made in high water, with two men at the sweeps all the time—the way the salt boats were run before the railroad came to the salt wells. The boat is run head on, and the oar and rudder sweep pins are worn bright by the navigators. In one place a four-foot dam would be jumped (Dickensons) and it might be necessary to run the boat around another on rollers, but this need not be a worrisome task if the boat is built of light, substantial wood.

There are cobblestone mill dams all the way

down the Alleghany Mountain rivers, and some of
them are not open to house-boat navigation.   High
water is essential, but water enough is had for log
rafts several times a year.   A cabin-boater on these
streams should consult the log raft pilots and get lists
of "bad places" by way of guide book.   No night run-

A Holston River Shoal.

ning should be thought of, and frequent stops along
the way should be made to inquire about the river.

The rivers have long shoals in them where the
water bounds along in picturesque fashion.   It is advisable to take a look at such waters before attempt-
ing to run them; snags and rocks being noted, and
particularly should the water at the foot of the shoals

be studied, for there disaster may be met when vigilance relaxes. Cloud Shoals and Mussel Shoals on the Tennessee are examples of tolerably bad water, the latter especially being in places exceedingly dangerous. But past the Mussel Shoal there is a government canal.

The beds of the mountain streams are fairly well fixed. Cut offs, caving banks, huge sandbars, etc., are hardly known. One does not have to seek "pockets" or sheltered places on these ridge-surrounded waters, unless there is a long reach of water where the waves might swamp, or a wind capsize a boat. But it must not be forgotten that the Tennessee is quite wide enough to make trouble for the careless cabin-boater, especially when the drift or ice is running. I've seen cabin-boats that were wrecked on it by the wind.

Exceedingly high water makes many dangers on all rivers, from the Mississippi to the Little Holston. Unless a boat is very strongly built, and has ample gunwale height, the racking from running shoals, or jumping wind waves will strain it without striking an obstruction. Cabin-boats are seen sometimes to fairly dissolve on the Mussel Shoals, perhaps with people in them, though no one can say as to that.

Some special dangers should be mentioned:

When the Mississippi is "out of its banks," the river is in places forty miles or more wide. The sweep of wind over such a breadth, though through the woods much of the way, raises a fearsome sea. When the water is high, all the pockets, chutes and other shelters are inundated, and one must tie to the levee itself, or find shelter next to the bank, back in the woods somewhere—from which last task the cabin-boater had better refrain.

The Mississippi Out of Its Banks—Shanty Boats Tied to Trees.

Care has to be taken on all the rivers in high water to keep from being thrust out of the current into woods where the boat would be smashed to driftwood at a single bump. The experienced man does not attempt to travel at such a time unless compelled to do so.

The lower Mississippi rises only a few inches a day. But its Alleghany headwaters jump up with frightful rapidity when heavy rain comes. Sometimes they rise five feet an hour and at the mouth of Little Holston the water comes up thirty feet in the course of a night. Naturally, under such conditions, short lines are not permissible for mooring, and trees, not stakes, are tied to with loose loops, not with half hitches. The Tennessee at the Alabama line will rise two or three feet a day, or more, but it does not come up with the rush its small feeders display.

Drift, on a narrow river, like the Holston, French Broad, or similar stream, must be thought about when a tide is coming. Rafts sometimes come grinding down, and any one log is heavy enough to smash in a boat's sides. If the water is rising, care should be taken to consider the chances of drift, and it will do no harm to always tie in sheltered nooks, of which all rivers have plenty.

Once in a while, on any river, whether the Hudson, or the Mississippi, or even the Erie Canal, it will be necessary to get up at night and change the lines or meet an emergency when cabin-boating. It was to help the cabin-boater prepare for these things that this was written.

The lower Mississippi does not freeze, but the upper waters all do and ice is something to be kept out of. If the cabin-boater is caught in a nip on any river, he should get his boat up the bank and wait for the ice to go out.

A special chapter on "Troubles" has been written and in this ice is discussed sufficiently. Also hints on climbing a bank with a houseboat are given.

The bayou rivers of the Mississippi Bottoms offer unique entertainment. In the swamps of Louisiana there are hundreds of miles of bayous—Grand River, Atchafayala, La Fouche, Courtebleau, etc., etc.,—through a region so wild and little known that most people have never heard of it. Starting at Vicksburg, one can drop down to the mouth of Red River, go up eight miles to Atchafayala and float down to Morgan City, Louisiana. If the Mississippi River is up, the current flows up Red River and down Atchafayala River. The current is very swift but not difficult to navigate. One goes down at such a rapid rate that the voyager is likely to find himself at the end of the journey almost before he realizes it is begun. On these bayous, in winter, rare enjoyment and sport is to be had, and all things considered, the small cabin-boater will not find a better region in the world for his first experience, than down Atchafayala.

A house-boater with a staunch craft will find numerous river-like streams around Chesapeake Bay, on which summer can be passed, working to and fro, with the tide or towing. From April to November, this region has advantages not to be ignored by houseboaters seeking "near-by" waters. Poor salt water boats, special paints, galvanized iron work, etc., are necessary in the boat construction. On these waters, sails, auxiliary power, and other approaches to yachts can be used with advantage, increasing as the boat grows in size. The scow hull gives way to the advantages of the model hull to some extent.

The cabin-boater should not forget that in river traveling his comfort decreases as the size of the boat increases. The ideal river journey boat is a skiff or canoe. If one puts a roof over a boat 15 feet long, and fits out accordingly, the little rivers are to be "house-boated"; though an auxiliary power, 90-footer could not get within five hundred miles of them. One handles a little cabin-boat just as easily as he does a skiff—it can even be carried around obstructions and toted overland on a truck, as from New Madrid across to the St. Francis.

The Hudson River has many cabin-boats on it, as well as more expensive house-boats. On it the sweeps give way to the sail, or gasoline tow. A boat must then be able to ride a severe storm and the craft is oftener anchored than tied to the bank.

Any bay of the Great Lakes, for instance, offers cabin-boating opportunity. One needs lee shelters on the wide waters, however, and one would better have a motor-boat than a cabin-boat on the Great Lakes. Down the St. Lawrence is famous house-boating water.

Now that there are good roads leading down to so many streams and lakes where a cabin-boat can be put afloat and moored or anchored, the boat held at one landing may have a hunting or trapping territory around it of a thousand square miles, merely by adding a motorcycle to the outfit, as has been remarked elsewhere. There is many a cabin-boater who takes the trolley car to his work, and I know of trappers that use railroad trains and trolleys, as well as motorcycles and bicycles in covering their lines. It would be quite feasible in countries where the roads are

11 C. B. P.

good late in the season and through the winter, to make many hundred miles of line for weekly covering.

Every invention that makes for easier communication makes for wider radius from a cabin-boat landing. If one camps on a little lake in a house-boat, every trail and road leading from it is part of his cabin-boat country, to be reached on foot and bicycle, motorcycle, or other conveyance. A house-boat may be transported from place to place if it is of the right size. At Dixon, Illinois, the Fines, husband and wife, built a boat about fifteen feet long which four men could carry around dams on the Rock River, if need be. Such a boat could be taken by wagon, train or steamer anywhere. With a little ingenuity, a small house-boat could be built that one could take down, pack and ship, and then set up again somewhere else.

The advantages of a house-boat are numerous— no other camp is quite so flexible with the same comforts and uses. The tent does not float, for instance— but a tent can be spread on a raft and hull. There is no play house for boys and girls who can swim and grown people quite so attractive as one that floats on a stream or lake.

CHAPTER XIV.

Maps and Landing Lists.

O N any river followed by steamboats, one can find lists of landings, how far apart they are and inquiry will disclose what to look out for in certain bends and reaches. The cabin-boater should make special effort to get these landing lists, for they will prove of great value.

Many of the large rivers have been mapped carefully and the cabin-boater should surely get the maps. The Mississippi River Commission has printed excellent maps of the Mississippi and many of its tributaries. One can travel down the St. Francis, Atchafayala, or other bottom land rivers by means of large maps, lists of which the commission will furnish.

The traveler must, however, travel by common state maps on some streams and most of the maps of states which one buys are merely useful in giving one a general idea in what part of the state he is. It is said that Americans are among the poorest in the world. For lack of better, the cabin-boater should have a state map, but if county surveys are to be had, they will be better yet as a rule.

The cabin-boater should always know where he is. Failure to keep track of bends on the Tennessee might lure him into the Suck or Mussel shoals unawares.

On the Ohio and Mississippi, the government maintains lights which indicate the channel. The maps show the river as it winds and flows, its sandbars, chutes, islands, obstructions, landings, etc., and

Storm Approaching — Water Rough.

lists of government lights are to be had of the river commissions which will be of great assistance to one who ventures to float by night, or by day.

When floating, the map is kept open on the table and watch of bank and map will quickly get one accustomed to locating himself immediately. The river map's value can scarcely be overestimated when one is seeking a snug landing, or some particular sandbar, where the wild geese feed. Many river cabin-boaters never use a map, and one must float "sight unseen" on some streams. Still, it is more than worth while to find out from the director of the United States Geological Survey whether the government or any department of the government has issued a map of the river in question.

Of course, the cabin-boater will have a compass with him. It is most desirable when one enters a canebrake, for example, and even in the back lots of a county, it is needful in keeping the direction of a landing in mind. In floating down a river, the course of the bed channel can be told by compass much more quickly than by the sun. If one happens to be caught in a fog or by night the compass and map will be of great value in keeping off a caving bank, or in making a good landing. By all means get the best possible maps.

Merely river maps should always be supplemented by road maps, showing in which directions roads and trails go, and if one can add to these maps notes and inscriptions indicating the character of the country, the maps are that much more valuable to the traveler. As I have elsewhere remarked, the cabin-boater is not only a water traveler; he is also a land traveler, and to get the best of his opportunities he must travel the land and the water both.

In order to travel on the Great Lakes, one needs more than a house-boat, of course, but St. Lawrence River, the waterways from Lake Huron to Lake Erie, and from White Fish Bay (foot of Lake Superior) to Lake Huron are all mapped, as well as the Great Lakes, and a letter addressed to the Superintendent of Documents, Washington, D. C., will bring descriptions of government maps of the waterways one desires to travel.

Too much emphasis could not be laid of the need of good maps, if any are to be had, for the traveler, whether on foot, by boat, or wheels. What is the use of civilization if one does not have good maps? Even when one is floating on a three-mile lake, a map of the surrounding country is worth having, and the surveys of the Geological Survey, Washington, D. C., have resulted in hundreds of maps that show various parts of the country in minutest detail—one can hunt deer by some of the woods maps of the survey, and save himself from being lost.

CHAPTER XV.

FLOATING.

ONE travels with the current in a cabin or house-boat and a great deal of the journey is made by simply letting the water carry the craft whither it will down the channel. Many a Mississippi shanty-boater casts loose from the bank and as soon as his boat is well in the current, he lies down to sleep knowing that his boat will keep in the main channel and not once in a thousand times, come to unheralded disaster. But the tyro cannot do this with safety, nor the cabin-boater of long experience always with impunity.

When one hears a steamer's huge paddles bucketing the water far down or up the stream, there is need of a look around, lest a huge tow of barges run one down, or a villianous pilot "play a joke" by swamping the house-boat with waves. There are a number of steamer pilots on the Mississippi who delight to make trouble for cabin-boaters and they would do it far oftener if they dared risk the rifle bullets which their victims send into the pilot houses of the criminal boats. The cabin-boaters on the Mississippi will tell the stranger what ones to look out for and among the rest are sure to be one or two of the government fleet. The chances are, however, that the tripper will not have the least trouble with the steamboats. They simply have to be thought of, among other things.

When in the wide current, the cabinboat is kept broadside to it. Obstacles are avoided by rowing across the river far enough to clear them. A landing is made by rowing toward the bank, starting far above the objective pocket, if one is near mid-stream. Because of its size and weight the cabinboat necessarily rows slowly and the current has a strong grip on the bottom. Wind, of course, makes a difference, to be explained further on.

Floating in ordinary weather and stage of the water may be made a matter of considerable science. If one is in a hurry, the boat is kept in the swiftest of the main current. Of two cabinboaters starting from St. Louis at the same time, skill in catching the current will make a difference of from ten to thirty miles a day in floating.

The swiftest water is ordinarily next to the caving bank. The slow water and large eddies are usually along the bars and at the foot. Rarely can one gain time by making a cut-off through a chute, for at the foot of a chute is often a long stillwater with scarcely any current in it. The government lights on the bank, standing on white posts, mark the channel and by keeping on the line between them the tyro will make fast time.

But speed is seldom desired by an ordinary tripper in a houseboat. The 1,200 miles from St. Louis to New Orleans is not a distance to be hurried over if one would make the most of it. Neither is any journey down the Tennessee, Cumberland, Ohio, Illinois, Arkansas, Red or other rivers to be made hastily, save under compulsion. One can, if he must, outrun the tide in a cabinboat, but it is better to pause here and there and take the whole breadth of what is at hand, than to skim down two shores, scarcely visiting them at any time.

If one lets the boat take its own time between the landings, the floating will be much the pleasanter.

The Mussel Shoals Canal.

Keeping exactly in the fastest current requires constant study of the river and a great deal of arm work at the sweeps. A stroke now and then is all that is necessary on a calm day from start to finish. One will sometimes float for hours without touching an oar. But a little neglect of lookout may result in the boat shunting into a huge eddy from which it may take an hour to pull out, as the one above Fort Pillow, below Yankee Bar, or the tremendous one at Vicksburg.

Of course, in smaller streams—in the upper Tennessee and on the Missouri—the cabinboater cannot be too watchful, nor his boat too handy in the water. Coming down Cloud Shoals, or any other Tennessee river rifts require both skill and nerve. Mussel Shoals should never be attempted, for the canal alone is safe. In an ordinary stage, the Suck, Frying Pan, etc., below Chattanooga under Lookout Mountain is not a hard proposition if one keeps in midstream and away from both banks. The Mississippi below St. Louis presents only a few quick, or bad water problems, the worst of which is at Grand Tower, which one must avoid at any cost, by keeping well away from the west side.

The falls of the Ohio at Louisville are guarded by government lifesavers, but in moderately high water they may be safely passed at the north bank by cabinboats. One should carefully study his maps and keep himself informed as to the river ahead of him in any of the swifter streams, such as the Tennessee or Cumberland. For a first trip cabinboating, only practically unbroken currents should be attempted, say the Hudson, Mississippi, Ohio and the salt still waters in lagoon countries.

There are a few things especially to look out for in the Mississippi—like currents. There are snags along the banks due to trees caving off. These snags whipping up and down in the swift water might cave the bottom of a boat in, or snatch off a cabin as it goes by. Keeping clear of them is simply a matter of rowing across the current.

In the shoal waters of a crossing, or along a bar, a root sometimes sticks up from the bottom, threatening to "hang" a boat. Even when considerably under the surface, the eye quickly discovers them by the incurling ripples below.

Occasionally, the cabinboater will be deceived by what looks like wide, deep waters, but proves to be a shoal of so little depth as to ground him. This is an embarrassing mishap, to avoid which the tyro will do well to take soundings in waters of different appearances, which will help him to learn the "looks" or reading, of the water. Under "The River" different aspects will be discussed with a view to helping the man afloat.

Save in time of necessity, don't try to float on a windy day. It can be done but it is a doubtful, disagreeable task, for one must always work to windward with his sweeps, save when the current happens to run down the lea—then a sail makes a boat travel, not like a bird, but with a satisfactory degree of speed from a cabinboater's standpoint. If one has a gasoline launch, the wind can be beaten usually, but the threat of a squall or cyclone, should always be respected with the utmost care. Steamers are sometimes blown against the bank by a gale.

If a little drift is running, the anxious cabinboater can make fast to a big snag, and the great weight will carry him into the wind, while the wide area of flotsam will break the waves. But the line should be made fast by a knot easily slipped from the boat deck, in case the drift starts for a drift pile, or enters a snaggy bend, like Plum Point Reef.

The cabinboater can float comfortably two or three days a week on the average. One can often float at night, though the days are much too windy, but night floating is treated under another chapter. Few souls are so hardy as to choose night floating rather than wait, however. Of this, mention is made in "Night and Day Floating."

A pair of good marine glasses are of great assistance in floating. The distances are too great to trust the naked eye on the best cabinboat waters. When dropping down on a group of islands, it is often essential that the route be chosen long before the naked eye would discover it. If one is seeking a landing, the glasses are practically indispensable, disclosing eddies, pockets, chutes, reefs, mud, sand and many other things essential to observe as the floating day comes to a close.

In making a chute, one should keep his boat fairly close to the bank—within fifty yards, say—until the chute is reached, and then the current will take one into it. But to keep clear of a chute, it is necessary to keep further out, for the draw of such a place sometimes reaches far into the main river. A houseboater, bound for New Orleans, would unquestionably be non-plussed to find himself sucked down the mouth of Red River toward Atchafayala bayou. And in the lower Mississippi, the traveler will do well not to mistake one of these huge delta streams for a mere chute behind an island.

If the ice is running, or the drift is coming heavy, venturing into the current is not to be thought of. Innocent as the ice and low-lying drift appears, it is a deadly danger, and a cabinboater so foolish as to go into it, is sure to go to grief where the stuff packs in some bend. Of course, there is nearly always a little drift coming down with the rising water, but this applies to the time when the black or gray mass is hundreds of feet, or yards wide and flows past in an unbroken mass.

Occasionally for the sake of company two cabinboats are lashed together for floating. With the bows side by side, the outside oars can be used in swinging the boats, but in case of emergency, the lines should be cast off. Sometimes the boats are lashed end to end, which allows the use of all the oars. Sometimes half a dozen boats are tied together, but this is only on calm days.

When floating, the skiff should always be ready for instant use, with the oars under the seat in the boat. The painter should be long enough to let it swing clear of the stern, but not so long as to let its *stern swing forward so as to interfere with the bow* oars. The best place for fastening the painter is on the stern steering oar pin (used only with a sail). If there are two tenders, they must be kept clear of each other, and when backing up, a look to see that the boats are not square across the stern is always an essential precaution.

Clumsy as the boat looks, and hard as the sweeps pull, one soon learns to float his house forty miles with less effort than walking through the woods a tenth that distance. But the fidgety, or nervous man, is almost sure to make too much work of his floating. Let the current manage the boat between landings and when there is a dispute between the wind and water, one would better wait till the current sends the craft close to some safe eddy, or chute and then, with a few strong strokes, drive the boat to shelter to wait for a better day.

CHAPTER XVI.

Floating at Night and in Fogs.

IT will sometimes happen that a cabinboater will wish to hurry down stream—perhaps his grub box is getting low, or he may be anxious to reach a better hunting territory, or get an open job. Then the wind will seem perverse, and the very river itself against him. But a cabinboater in a hurry usually gets there on time if he is ingenious and has his nerve. A woman has been known to float from Cairo to Vicksburg, without tying a line for wind, fog, night or anything else, but she knew the river and how to meet its moods.

Fog is worse than night, for at night one has the government lights. With map and compass the cabinboater may get down stream in a fog, but it isn't a good plan to try it. A steamer may happen along, or one may strike the head of a tow of barges, which means at best a jump for life. Still, steamers usually tie when a fog comes up, lest they come to grief on snags or sand bars.

If the water is falling the cabinboat is reasonably certain to keep in the river channel if there is no wind, hence the cabinboater can make time by trusting to the current. A lookout must be kept, however, lest one hit a snag or strike a bad shallow, or be sucked into a chute, of which the map will give one warning. The compass and knowledge of the probable speed of the current will help one keep track of directions, and whether a bend is being made safely or not. The ears will warn one when the boat is approaching a caving bank or snags. To some extent, the appearance of the water around the boat will help one keep track of himself. Of course, if his map has soundings on it, he can keep informed as to his position to some extent. Even with no idea of the water, he can tell whether he is getting into shoal water or not and if the current is swift or not by the way the bottom snatches the pole or lead back.

Night traveling is considerable better than fog traveling. At night by keeping one's boat on the line between the government lights on the Mississippi and Ohio, the channel is kept. Sharp lookout must be kept for steamers and tows and a lantern should be kept on the roof where it can be seen by any pilot. All other lights on board should be extinguished, lest they confuse the floater's eyes and prevent his keeping track of bends and reaches or catch sight of bad water ahead.

Night floating is nerve-trying work and yet there are Mississippi cabinboaters who usually travel at night. They stick a lantern on the roof, cut loose and go to bed. They are reasonably certain to be awakened by a coming steamer, or roused by the wind. But it is not a sure or a safe way of traveling. One cabinboater told me how he had cut loose and thought he had floated all night, but in the morning he had found himself in the same eddy from which he had started. All night long the boat had gone around and around in the whirl. It took the man an hour to recognize the place.

By night or in a fog, everything is changed in its appearance. Land looks to be far away and nearby objects loom up in gigantic fashion. Noises are much plainly audible—in fact, the river seems a vastly different place.

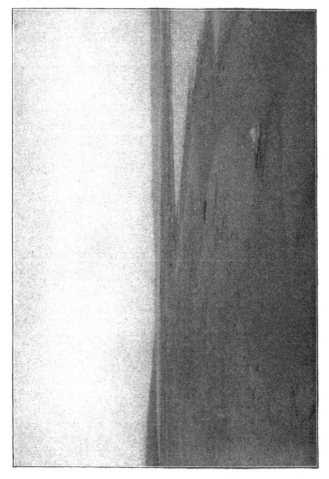

The Sand Bar

It is better not to attempt to go afloat in the fog under any circumstances, nor at night, unless daytime navigation has been mastered, and then not unless one has good night glasses, plenty of nerve and an agile wit in an emergency. A tendency to panic is very difficult to curb in the darkness.

Of course, no one will think of floating down mountain streams at night. Wind affects a boat on narrow waters but little and the cabinboater will find that in the long run the fewer chances taken, the more enjoyment there is to be had in the journey.

CHAPTER XVII.

Going Up Stream.

THE cabin-boater is not likely to do much up-stream work. If he wishes to save his boat for another trip, one can get a tow from some steamer or other, if the cabin-boat will stand the racking. It will cost a cent or two a mile usually to tow up stream.

If one has a gasoline boat, up-stream work can be done to advantage very often, for a little power will do wonders against a slow current. If one can afford it, a several horsepower launch can be made to do a great deal of desirable up-stream cross-current work.

It will occasionally happen that a cabin-boater will want to work up stream for a little ways. There are so many tempting branches coming into most rivers that a little side trip is almost sure to be attempted up one or another of them. In any event one is certain to wish to go against an eddy's flow or a chute's draw sooner or later.

One can make little or no headway against a current with the sweeps. Ropes must be called into play, or at least poles on the bottom. The old-time keel-boater had running boards along both sides of his craft. With long poles set on the bottom, he walked aft and thus thrust the boat up stream. Some few cabin-boats have running boards on to this day, but they are rarely seen on the rivers.

The long handyline can be run up the stream and made fast to a tree or log, or dropped overboard, fastened to an anchor. Then by hauling it in, hand over hand, the boat is drawn up stream.

It is possible in many places for a man to cordell —hitch a line to a bulkhead and walk up the bank with the other end. I have seen a large cabin-boat on its way up the Tennessee with one man towing it up. The boat had been worked up stream a hundred or more miles in easy stages, advantage being taken of reverse eddies and dead waters.

In up-stream work a sail is sometimes of value.

If one takes a notion to go up the Mississippi River, bayous or rivers, there are many gasoline boats whose owners would gladly take the tow as far as desired, and the price is likely to be fair. Having made the trip up, coming back is a simple enough matter if one doesn't get caught in low water.

Of course, if one has his own gasoline boat, it is easy enough to tow one's own boat up stream, and the expense in gasoline or whatever is burned in the motor, is not great. Yet where one must count the cost, it is always best to work down stream, rather than up. If one intends to start from and return to a certain landing, it is best to go up stream and float back, rather than go down stream and tow back. It is always astonishing to a man making his first trip down stream to find how far he goes down and how long it takes to pull back up stream. For a day's picnic, it is better to go up stream in the morning and come down in the afternoon than to go down stream in the morning and come up in the afternoon, supposing, of course, that one has not got a reliable motorboat.

CHAPTER XVIII.

WEATHER.

THERE are some weather signs which it is good to know if one would go cabin-boating on the Mississippi. Ordinarily, wind comes in periods. One will have a day or two of calm, then a day of fitful breezes lasting from 9 or 10 o'clock till mid-afternoon. The breeze gusts will come earlier next day and still earlier the next and with increasing strength and steadiness until an all-day gale is blowing. But at sundown the wind dies away. The wind, in these periods, is usually from the south, on the Mississippi. Sometimes this wind blows up a rain, or perhaps a shift brings a cold wave from the north after three or four days. The nights are oftener more calm than the day.

While light winds are drifting hither and yon, the sky will frequently reveal the coming of a wind change worth foretelling, especially on wide water. When the filmy clouds are driving slowly toward any quarter and begin to spread out fan-like over the leeward sky, it means the zephyrs have met an adverse current —and that adverse current, driving against the zephyrs, is coming to change the direction of the wind— the wind will be from the direction where the spreading out occurs.

Sometimes calm, warm weather in the south, is followed not by winds, but by a gradual thickening of the air. Clear, beautiful sunshine gives way to increasing haze and after a time the sun fades from view. Suddenly, after a few hours or few days, stray

(180)

catspaws of wind come slapping through the haze.
This is a good time to look out—to fly for shelter in
a chute or eddy where one can ride a gale, or cyclone.
The gusts come with increasing strength and then
with a roar, a frightful storm leaps out of the murk
and fairly whips the river surface into foam. Such
storms have been known to turn cabin-boats clear over
and to set others high and dry on sand bars or flat
beaches. Heavy boats are usually the ones that are
upset, light ones merely ride the waves and toss about.
Unless strongly built, the cabin of the boat may be
lifted from the hull.

The cyclones sometimes come up in the open on
a clear day. They are seen afar at such times, and it
is worth while keeping an eye on the horizon when one
isn't in shelter. A warm day will disclose a little
cloud, "like a hand," to the west or south, usually.
A second look shows that it has grown perceptibly
and the third time one sees a black mass where a filmy
blue speck had appeared. This is a good time to
work up to the windward bank under shelter of the
land. Across the face of the blue cloud, and reaching
high into the sky are long white streamers of cloud—
very pretty to look at, and suggesting waving white
plumes.

In the meanwhile, the birds have stopped singing,
and waterfowl spring from their feeding places at
the points of the sand bars and fly to the little ponds
back in the willows. Absolute silence ensues—a
silence that often attracts the attention of cabin-
boaters to what is coming.

The clouds, black, threatening, and fairly boiling,
pour up into the sky. Rain and hail come in gusts.
Away up to windward a gray mist appears. It sweeps
along, enveloping trees and buildings in its gloom.

One catches glimpses of trees bending to the blast and then they fade from view. If the way happens to be over a sand bar, one sees the gray turn sullenly to a wonderful yellow as the sand is sucked a thousand feet toward the zenith. In a few seconds one is dancing to the ropes and glancing anxiously about, wondering if everything is going to hold.

The first blast gone by, the wind sometimes lays, but usually the wind continues for many hours with considerable violence. The warm, even hot, weather gives way to almost a freeze or to a temperature 20 of 50 degrees colder than that at the beginning of the storm.

One can very often learn much from the actions of the birds. When a cold spell is coming, the wild fowl race southward before it, the greatest activity being noticeable the day before it arrives. The blue herons are especially worth noticing. When one sees them piking southward as fast as they can go, it means bad weather—sometimes a prolonged freeze.

Filmy clouds, like dust, usually called maiden tresses, rising slowly but perceptibly out of the west, usually means hard wind for the following day— that is, too hard for floating.

Fog driven by wind, means rain coming, though mere flat fog indicates fair weather for a while. Whiffs of fog, coming and going, indicate wet weather in prospect. An east wind generally means rain. If birds call unusually loud, especially cormorants, geese on sand bars, and ducks, the cabin-boaters say warm rains are in sight.

When a fog comes falling down through the trees and onto the river surface, it is a sign of rain; but when it rises, it means clear weather. A heavy frost means clear weather.

Warm streaks in a fog indicate pretty weather. A red sunset is regarded as a promise of wind.

The chief value of reading the weather signs is knowing when bad storms of wind are coming. One should hunt shelter from cyclonic storms, which the weather foretells. It is also a good thing to keep away from open sand bars if the wind is going to blow, for the sand is carried far by a dry gale, making cabin-boat life a sorrow, rather than a joy.

Cabin-boaters become weather prophets naturally, and it pays to study the signs.

The best time of year to go afloat in a cabin-boat depends on the river. The upper Missouri is a summer country, the lower Mississippi a winter resort. I should say September woud be a good time to start from St. Louis or Pittsburg. The upper Tennessee and Holston is never more beautiful than in September or October, and summer in the Alleghenies is far from unbearable.

The Great Lakes waters are summer boating for the cabin-boater, motor-boater and skiff man.

Erie Canal House Boats.

CHAPTER XIX.

Making Fast and Some Rope Hints.

THE cabin-boater is a sailor—"a genuine, home-comfort" navigator. He should know how to splice ropes and make various knots, yet I have seen shanty-boaters who made fast with a trot line to sticks eighteen inches long driven into loose sand, tying a slip knot which would pull out if the boat strained it. Once I traveled on the Mississippi River with a medicine man who had two-inch cables with which to fasten a 30-foot boat to the bank. His knots were heaps of rope, square, granny, and slip, some one of which was sure to hold, whatever became of the others. The regulation stake knot is two half hitches, and a bight around the line. This will hold in any gale, and as long as the stake and rope holds.

In making a landing, the boat comes bow on to the bank. The up-current bow line is run ashore to a stake, tree or log and made fast. Sometimes, if the current is strong, both the bow and stern up-current lines are run out, and made fast, to keep the bow and stern from swinging down the current. Then the down-current lines are made fast down the bank. (Fig. 1.)

Last of all a stake is driven opposite the middle of the bow bumper and the gangplank braced against it. The rope at the other end of the plank is tied to the cleat on the bow bumper, with a few inches slack line for "play."

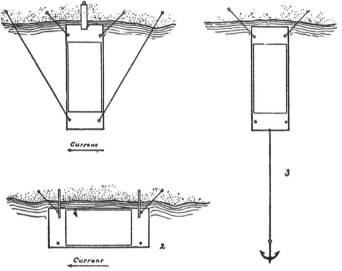

Modes of Tying Up a House Boat.

Another way of making fast is most serviceable in a narrow eddy or a swift current. The bow is run to the bank, the down-stream bow line run to a stake or tree and made fast. The boat swings broadside around to the bank and the stern line taken ashore and made fast. (Fig. 2.)

In a broadside landing, it is a good plan to spar the boat away from the bank by running out the gangplank at the bow and lashing it to the timberhead or oar pin. Once in a while it may be necessary to spar off the stern as well. If the anchor is thrown out a few fathoms and the stern hauled out by the anchor line and made fast, a long spar will be unnecessary.

If the wind is driving the boat to the bank, dropping the anchor over the stern and paying out forty or fifty feet before the bow gets to the bank, then snubbing up and making fast to the bank with the bow lines will serve to keep the boat bow-on to the bank. The two stern bank lines need not be run ashore then. (Fig. 3.)

If one is going into a wide, shoal eddy, it is often advisable to drop the anchor over the stern in deep water. This will not only serve to hold the boat from pounding the bank, but if the water should fall, leaving the boat aground, the boat can be hauled off by means of the anchor line.

Very often, even in a narrow eddy, with tolerably deep water astern, it is advisable to have the anchor out, for nothing will so well keep a boat from pounding against the bank in a gale. The gangplank will serve well enough in a breeze, but in a norther, or a cyclonic storm, the anchor, even two anchors, is needed.

If the anchor happens to drag deep into the soft mud, the slack will have to be taken in from time to time. And when one is ready to hoist the anchor, it must be done by starting the boat over the hold, catch the line around the cleat and jerk the anchor loose. If the anchor happens to catch under a log, it is likely to be lost, unless one has a tight line tied to one of the flukes. This tight line will hoist the anchor out of almost any kind of fastening.

Always keep the ropes coiled when not in use. The handyline especially should be kept ready for instant service somewhere in the cabin out of the wet. Long hooks on the ends of the cabin are useful to hang the mooring lines and anchor cable over, up out of the way of one's feet on the deck.

CHAPTER XX.

A COMPLETE discussion of Mississippi and other river landings is of course out of question here. But some hints as to what kind of landings to choose for stops are worth giving. It is essential that the novice give the subject of landings considerable thought.

Broadly speaking, there are three things to consider in making a landing—the wind, drift and ice, and caving banks.

The west and south winds must always be reckoned with, but a gale may come from any direction. Still, if one lies under the lee from the west and south, the first principle of cabinboating is followed.

Along both sides of a river are countless eddies, some of them a mile long and very wide and some mere swirls under a bank. If one is in deadwater or in a slow eddy, out of reach of long arms of rapidly-moving tree trunks, he is safe from drift, but if he happens to be caught in a narrow eddy by the grinding ice pack, or pounding drift, his boat is likely to be doomed by crushing. A single log, driving down in low water, may strike an unsheltered boat such a blow as to wreck it; hence the need of at all times making landings safe from drift and ice.

One is not apt to tie in under a caving bank. The very appearance of such a place is likely to warn a cabinboater to be wary and keep away. And yet, one must occasionally take refuge from the water by coming into such shelter as land that is constantly threat-

(188)

ening to fall into the water affords. A bank which is falling before ones eyes, is of course, to be avoided at any cost, but there are banks which are not slipping and may not slip for months. The eye quickly identifies these and one will often find his best shelter from storms and rift in the ragged shore line of a bank whose forest is on the brink of destruction.

Tied in a pocket on the Missouri or Mississippi with the current whistling by not ten yards astern, a cabinboat may lie safely for weeks, but the cabinboater will do well to drive stakes, rather than tie to fallen.trees. If the bank should suddenly start to sliding into the river some night, it would be far easier to haul in the stakes than to save the ropes from huge snags. A log, too, might pull a boat so far over as to endanger its safety.

In a journey down a Mississippi basin river, lasting several months, the cabinboater will tie in at nearly every kind of a landing, of course. On occasion he will even risk a west wind against a caving bank, but not for long. As he grows more experienced, he will hunt shelter more and more. The joy of his heart will be a chute sheltered from wind and drift, a snug and cosy berth which he will leave with regret, and the like of which he will hunt for many hours, rather than land on the wide river.

A chute behind an island is ideal, but they are not always to be had, especially in low water. As a rule, the higher the water, so long as it is not out of its banks, the better the landings one can find.

If one is caught in a hard wind, it is better to be driven on a sandbar than against a caving bank. The worst of a sandbar is, that if the river is falling, one may be hung up, high and dry, while a caving bank many sink or break a boat. Under "Troubles" will be

Memphis, Tenn., Shanty Boat Town.

found a discussion of this phase of river life. A thirty or forty-pound anchor, or mud hook, will hold one off a sandbar, or even caving bank, though in the latter case a long line is usually necessary—perhaps two or three hundred feet or more. If the river is rising, a cabinboat will soon float clear of a bar. While waiting for the water to rise, it is best to be tied to a stake or have an anchor out on the sand.

Very quickly the eyes will be accustomed to selecting places to land which will be safe. Carelessness is alone to be feared then. Cabinboating is not a pastime in which to take chances.

In three days, the eye should recognize the "old bank" not likely to cave, the caving bank, the shoal water and the muddy landing. Better land against a steep bank in an eddy than against the mud of a flat. An old river fisherman selected his landing just above Helena, Ark., against an exposed sand reef at the head of the long Helena eddy. The water was shallow and under the boat was mud. The sand made good footing for going ashore to split wood and hold the driven stakes and the mud was soft for the boat to pound on. When high water came, he ran into Helena chute, where a pocket in the bank preserved his little boat from every harm.

There is usually a good landing place at the foot and at the head of a sandbar. At these places there is always an eddy in which will break the waves from the river current. Moreover, the bank is likely to be good. But if it is a long, dry, naked sandbar, beware of the wind. Of all places to weather a gale, the lee side of a mile of loose sand is the most uncomfortable and disagreeable. The sand blows through the cracks of the tightest boat and fills everything with grit. A bar grown to willows, however, makes as good a landing as any to be had.

In February, when the ice runs out of the Ohio, or at any time when the drift or ice is coming, preparation should be made, with every care, for the passing of the pack. One would better get into a snug chute. In any event, a long, still eddy had better be chosen. The drift comes down the river like a long snake, and the wind drives it to windward, sometimes filling the little eddies. Many a cabinboat is thus destroyed and every year thousands of dollars' worth of barges are torn loose from their fastenings by the ice. Not even the steamers escape. When the cabinboater hears that the ice or drift is coming, he had better hunt a bayou, old lake or chute. At such times the debris is likely to cut into any caving bank, and wear away any "pocket" in a long bend. Of course, a bay at the foot of a sandbar is safe and all the big eddies offer refuge, so long as the current is not a strong one.

In making landings, the hunting, fishing, trading, trapping, and other matters will engage attention. Cabinboaters will frequently run every risk in order to make money or to have a good time. Across the river from Cairo (a city ordinance forbids landing shanty boats against the city bank) dozens of cabinboats are along the Kentucky bank, yet a hard west wind invariably swamps several of them and as many as twenty-five or thirty are swamped there in hard storms. Friar's Point, Luxora, Arkansas City, Helena, Memphis, and many other town landings are noted for the cabinboats that have been wrecked there. Yet up or down stream from these "landings" sometimes not half a mile distant, perfectly safe places are to be found. The cabinboat residents at Memphis invariably seek shelter in Wolf River, or Ash Slough,

House Boats at Greenville, Mississippi.

while at Greenville, they build skids on which to keep their boats on land in all but the highest waters.

A very little experience will assist the traveler to pick his landings from the river maps issued by the Mississippi River commission at 5 cents a sheet. The scale is an inch to the mile, and every landing, chute, sandbar, clearing, woodlot, and what not within a mile of the river is shown on these maps. No one should undertake a river journey without a good map, and especially should one have the commission's maps on the Mississippi, though a complete set from St. Louis to New Orleans costs five or six dollars. They issue maps of a great many rivers.

Most river men will tell a fellow cabinboater about good places to hunt, fish and where one may expect good "bank" neighbors. One should not forget that many bends are "owned" by fishermen who protect their claims with guns, and many trappers "own" certain excellent fur-yielding stands. Thieving shantyboaters have made some landings uncomfortable by their depredations on the bank people. In stopping at a regular landing, it is always well to make the acquaintance of other cabinboaters, or of the landing-keeper there.

If one does not care for company, stopping at the heads of long points and in wooded bends will keep him lonely enough to suit any hermit. There are men afloat on the Mississippi who do not speak to their kind once a week, if as often, while on the other hand, many cabinboaters make their trips from St. Louis to New Orleans a continuous round of gaiety. They are known in every shanty-boat town, and their arrival in any one, whether at the mouth of old Arkansas, or in a new saw-mill camp, is a signal for a good time.

Now of course, as regards wind, one must watch out on lakes, even small lakes, if he has a house boat. A very little blow across wide water will kick up a smashing sea, as regards the unwieldy square-bowed scow. It is better to haul the boat up the beach, clear of the waves than to try to ride any storm, and if one cannot find a good bay to tie in it is better to keep right on going in a cabinboat till a safe harbor is found, no matter whether on small lake or large river. There is hardly any boat less sea-worthy than a shanty-boat out of its place. Yet in its own waters—harbors and bays of small size, and rivers, there is no safer boat to be had. It is easy enough to know what is safe and what is not. Of course, a power house-boat, with high sides and tight, will ride as big a sea as any boat of its size—but that brings us into the realms of motorboats.

CHAPTER XXI.

TROUBLES.

THE true cabin-boater is also a philosopher. Troubles come to mean something in the way of a cause for congratulation rather than dismay. The writer and a medicine man were caught in an eddy at Salem landing above Vicksburg by a cyclone one afternoon. The first blast ripped off half the roof and while we danced to swing the boat astern to the gale on the anchor line the rain saturated all our bedding. For nine hours thereafter one pumped, because the waves dashed over the stern threatening to fill the boat, while the other saved the wreck of the roof, patched it and spread tarpaulin over the holes. From a warm summer-like day the temperature changed to just freezing. We filled our two stoves with wood, got down the still dry banjo and took out the French harp and played and sang away the shivers, and the trial, between our spells at the pump, at the lines and at the other things needful, while the wind swung from the west to the northeast, pounding us steadily from every point till long after midnight. From an occasion of distress, the buoyancy which life on the river in a cabin-boat gives one roused us to a point of genuine elation and merrymaking. What was real disaster became also an occasion of real joy, not to be forgotten in a day.

This will be the experience of the people who go afloat in house-boats in the Mississippi basin, or in other rough places. The most pleasant experiences will likely enough be associated with dire troubles. I have heard men relate with unfeigned glee how they were "tore up" at such a landing, or landed high and dry on such a barge. So far as I know, the unadulterated trial and sorrow on the river is the ruin of one's most cherished photograph films or plates. Besides this disaster, wreck of cabin-boat, theft of gun or money, night of cold and wet fade into insignificance. Against this every precaution should be taken—the plates and films kept in water-tight packages, wrapped with oilcloth with a convenient handle by which to carry them. The camera is little compared to the pictures of a month or so afloat. A camera can be replaced, but not a set of pictures.

Reasonable care should be taken to ward off trouble. Always find a good landing, as regards wind and water. Always keep both eyes open when floating and never take chances willingly. Never tie to a wobbly stake; never let the wood pile or oil can get low. Always keep the lantern filled and trimmed and hung on its own hook. Watch the fire and shut up the stove when leaving it, for a cabin-boat may burn.

Study the maps, question every cabin-boater about the river below and watch for snags, dodge the shoals and snaggy bends.

Above all things, perhaps, keep every rope in its place, with the end hanging down from the hook far enough to be instantly at hand. The anchor should be handy at the stern, with one end of a long stern line tied to it, ready for heaving overboard in case the boat starts for some place not desired, as before a gale into a mud bank.

The handy line, coiled neatly in a box indoors, should be ready to put into service at all times. If caught in a storm, this line may save the boat from going into a caving bank by hooking the anchor into the bottom in deep water. In driving toward an undesirable sand or mud bar, the stern line will serve the same purpose.

Once in a great while a sawing snag will give the boat such a thump as to break it in. If water makes fast, find the leak though the axe ruins half the floor. Perhaps a sprung board can be knocked back into place enough for the boat to make the nearest sand bar, or perhaps pieces of board can be nailed over the break—even a mattress or quilts from the bed may serve to keep the water out till the craft is grounded in shoal water.

If the river is going down, grounding on sand simplifies matters somewhat. When the bottom is out of water, the boat can be pried up with wedges of wood, laid on plank, and the boat tilted enough to put in new bottom boards or to patch.

If the boat cannot be saved on the water, put the valuables into the skiff or launch, make the two stern lines fast to the nigger-heads, so they won't slip—half hitches and a turn around the line. By these two lines, the half sunken hulk can be worked into an eddy. A deep, still eddy at the head or foot of a sand bar, or even a small eddy in a long bend will serve for the purpose. A caving bank will hardly do at all, lest a lumping off sink the boat.

With the boat close to land, the long handy line, with double or treble sheaves blocks will serve to hoist the boat high enough to let the water drain out and some sort of temporary repair made. A sheet of painted canvas or tarpaulin will sometimes serve to keep the water out of the hull if drawn under it with stout lines and tied fast over the cabin, or at the bulkhead.

Saving a sinking cabin-boat is not easy, but in such a task the tyro will sometimes find himself doing feats of which he never dreamed. And if he has a small boat he will bless his stars that it is not a large one, when this time of peril comes. A boat of small size, all things considered, is less troublesome than a large one. It is easier saved in time of storm or drift and it is easier handled when trouble does overtake it.

Getting aground on falling water is a misfortune of considerable moment. If the water is very low the boat should be jacked up and skids, mere boards, or logs, or poles put under it to raise it to an even keel, and then high water can be waited for with patience, especially if the near-by woods are full of game and wild geese and ducks feed along the edges of the bar.

But some waters mean weeks of waiting for their return. In that case the boat must be worked to the water over the sand. Slipping over mud is not a job to be undertaken lightly, easy as it sounds. If the boat is light, a railway of logs is laid and the boat shoved afloat on rollers. If there is any uphill work, the Spanish windlass may be necessary.

The Spanish windlass consists of a pole seven or eight feet long and five or six inches in diameter. One end is sharpened. Then a sapling or arm ten or twelve feet long is cut strong enough to bear a man's weight without too much bending. A short length of stout rope is wrapped around the big pole, or drum, often enough so it won't slip, and the arm thrust into a loop in the rope. A tow line or haul line, is led to the cabin-boat and made fast to two niggerheads at the end and the other end of the tow line is wrapped around the drum. One man holds to the drum, pointed end in the dirt, and the other, at the end of the arm, walks around and around, winding up the tow line. On a fair runway a very heavy cabin-boat can be moved in this way. Of course, a team of mules can usually be hired to set the boat afloat.

It is a good plan to patch the seams of a boat, especially if one is taking on a cargo. The gunwales dry out and if one doesn't look alive the boat may get deeper than a seam, upon which disaster may come. Old rope, bits of cloth, even grass, will serve for caulking, but of course it is better to have a wad of real oakum aboard for emergencies.

If being driven ashore by the wind, drop an anchor and ride out the storm.

One must expect to be seasick if one has any tendencies that way, but one soon becomes accustomed to the water rocking. Let the patient travel by easy stages, going ashore when the lonesome feeling comes. A little bank camp may be advisable for a time, for which a tent is worth having.

The Missisippi is sometimes swept by cyclones, which are gales of tremendous strength and consider-able danger. They usually come out of the south or west, but occasionally from other directions. A good eddy breaks the force of the waves they raise, but sometimes the wind hurls the whole river current against the bank, in which case the cabin-boater is in trouble. The cyclone usually foretells itself and in cyclonic weather the cabin-boater would better go into a chute and wait for the days to pass.

If caught in midstream by a sudden gale, the boat must be kept head on if possible. The anchor at the end of a long line—so long that the down pull of the rope will not draw the boat under—serves the purpose. The handy line should be strong enough for this emergency. Two stern mooring lines, tied together will be long enough in ordinary water, but if the boat is going into a caving bank the water is likely to be scores, if not hundreds of feet deep. A sea anchor, such as the stage plank, a tub or several buckets may gain time, if not save actual disaster. Ordinary wash tub handles are not strong enough to stand the strain, but reinforced by loops of rope over the bottom the tub may hold. Most boats use half a pork barrel for a wash tub and one of these, or even a wash boiler, or a several-gallon lard can, will materially check a boat's headway as it drives before the wind.

The cyclone blasts are often of brief duration, though of terrible severity while they last. The first five minutes usually decides the fate of the boat and if the cabin-boater is always ready for an emergency of the kind while traveling down the rivers, having something strong enough for sea anchor, besides the iron anchor, a wind storm need have but few terrors for him. Only, of course, it is far better to reserve traveling until a future date rather than risk a gale which might blow a top-heavy boat clear over, or drive it into a caving bank.

Sometimes the water drops unexpectedly and leaves the boat on the bottom too heavy to be shoved off by polling. If everything is moved to the end that is afloat, the opposite end can sometimes be lifted clear. But if this fails, or if the whole bottom is in the mud, one can take out the anchor in the skiff— two anchors, if one has them, and they are necessary. These are dropped overboard and a round log dropped behind the niggerheads, the ropes wound around it and handles thrust into holes in the sides of the log with the 1½-inch auger. The log, or drum, is then turned, the rope wound up and the boat drawn to the anchors. It is an adaptation of the Spanish windlass.

Sometimes a cabin-boater wants to get his boat up the bank on to a skid. A freeze, nipping his not-too-strong-sided boat, may threaten or be at hand. A moderate-size house-boat can nearly always be drawn out of the water by careful use of ropes around the hull, fast to the niggerheads and windlass. A light boat can be drawn up the bank on a runway and rollers by a team or two of horses, or by sheer man-power at a Spanish windlass rigged behind two trees. Cabin-boaters prepare to bank their boats by building a skidway on the bank and then floating over them in high water and waiting for the flood to go by, leaving them high and dry. At Greenville, Mississippi, some cabin-boats are twenty feet up the bank, on skids ten feet high. If one is going to stop awhile in a moun-tain community, it is just as well to take advantage of a moderately high water to land the boat. The next high water will probably float it, and, in any event, the right kind of a cabin-boat can always be slipped down the bank and into the water, like a turtle.

But a boat hull dries out when exposed to the air and it should be carefully caulked when dried out, otherwise the boat will almost surely fill when the water gets to the seams.

Sleet storms are frightful in the middle South. The water freezes to everything it touches and weighs down the trees, caves in the houses and kills the wild life. The cabin-boater must watch out for these storms and when it comes he can do no better than keep a hot fire going all night. This will tend to melt the ice from the cabin. But if it fails to melt the ice, the stuff must be kept chopped off, otherwise the hundreds of pounds of weight will sink or capsize the boat. It is better to scale the ice off at intervals than to have this happen. One should also be careful that the boat is not under a tree, or branches, the falling of which would break in the cabin-boat.

Many a boat has been wrecked by a wind or ice-felled tree.

Along some rivers, most small ones in fact, the cabin-boater need not worry about thieves, but a house-boat tempts the cupidity of many a river rat along the Ohio and Mississippi. On these rivers one cannot leave his boat alone for any length of time and caution must be taken that a thief does not come in the night and float away with the skiff or gasoline launch. The river rats are experts with little log dugouts, and they come and leave in silence unbroken.

Moreover, the friendship of a river rat, or river tramp, or river beggar is not to be cultivated. The river thief is the most treacherous of bad men. They have been known to come out of a storm and beg for shelter. Getting the confidence of a cabin-boater, or at least shelter on a boat, they took the first opportunity to steal away with everything valuable. They even kill their benefactors, and having dropped the bodies overboard, go on down the river in the boat. Ordinarily the river man is an interesting and peaceable citizen, but caution should be observed in becoming intimate with river strangers.

Life in a cabin-boat is very close to nature. It is akin to pioneering. The troubles are like the troubles of camping. The spirit in which they are received has much to do with one's enjoyment on the river, just as other outdoor troubles become pleasures or anxieties. Courage is the cabin-boater's best virtue, just as it is any other sportsman's.

A South Missouri Stream.

CHAPTER XXII.

CARE OF THE BOAT.

THE ordinary cabin-boater has learned the necessity of having everything in its place and everything clean. Floors are mopped, bedding aired, damp corners kept clean, and exposed to the sun or at least aired.

The hold of the boat should not be allowed to get musty. There should be some provision made for airing it frequently, if not all the time. Sliding hatches in the bow and stern decks will do this. When the floor is lower than the deck—it usually is—there should be little doors which will permit airing out the bow and stern, rather than deck hatches. Nothing soggy or wet should be thrust into these cubby holes "to get them out of the way." A box fastened to the roof will carry such things better. The junk man always has a large, shallow box on the roof for bones, rubbers, etc., etc.

Keeping the hold dry saves the wood, of course. It also preserves the health of the occupants.

If one buys a boat second-hand, a thorough house cleaning, painting and renovating generally will go far toward making the craft comforting and the same thing done at intervals will add greatly to a boat's selling price.

Repairs should be well made. Caulking should be done rather than pumping every day or two.

If the roof leaks ever so little, the matter should be attended to at once. Tarred paper is cheap, tar is cheap and any hole can be quickly fixed with a combination of tar and tarred paper, or canvas. If the roof is canvas, an occasional coat of white lead and oil will keep it in splendid condition. Tar can be used for the same purpose, but the sun on a tarred roof makes a boat very warm.

On a falling river, watch must be kept to see that the boat does not come down on a snag or get on the bottom. Care should be taken to see that the boat is tied where it will not rub its paint off, or projecting limbs punch through the cabin.

The hold should be examined frequently, lest some leak has started unawares. The ears, grown accustomed to river noises, should always be alert for the wash of water in the hold and the pound of a snag against the bottom. The eyes must ever be on the lookout for slipping knots, loosening stakes, fraying ropes and other things looking toward troubles.

A boat, that, with good care, would last for years, may go to pieces through carelessness. Nowhere does a stitch in time save so many stitches as on a cabin-boat.

If there is any gasoline or motor aboard the boat, the tanks and oil should be watched very carefully, and any leaks taken care of right away. An oil-soaked boat burns in a flash, and sometimes it explodes first.

Good Hunting and Fishing — Cattaraugus Creek, near Lake Erie.

CHAPTER XXIII.

Ways of Making Money.

THE would-be cabin-boater may well consider the money-making opportunities offered by a river journey. On every house-boat stream one will find chances for picking up expenses and even good profits. The cabin-boater of the Mississippi basin nearly all make their living while they journey from landing to landing. Some are sheer swindlers, making fake medicine and running the gauntlet of police supervision until finally reaching "The Farm," or other penal institution. The legitimate crafts are more numerous and of course in the long run far more profitable.

The most attractive project is the storeboat. A stock of groceries, cloth, hardware and other general merchandise laid in. Dropping from landing to landing, the goods are disposed of to customers attracted by the blowing of a horn and flying of a flag. The places distant from stores are best for trade, of course, but the store-boater, selling at reasonable prices, draws much trade from the "Commissaries" on the bank which most of them overcharge. There are dozens of store-boats on the rivers, some of them known favorably down long stretches of territory.

Many a man starts from St. Louis, Pittsburg, Evansville and other cities with scarcely a day's provisions on board his boat. By careful selection from river drift piles, sand bars, farm waste heaps, and anywhere a load of junk is picked up that at Cairo, Memphis or any other city, will bring day wages. Bottles, iron, brass, copper, bones, rubber, etc., etc., have a market value of which junkers afloat take advantage and make hundreds of dollars a trip. In this connection, it should be noted that old cotton gins, distilleries, refineries, etc., contain tons of metal which the junker can often get on contract, or by purchase, and float away to market with profit. Even if one is on a mere pleasure trip, odds and ends of brass fully pay the cost of the boat and even the expenses of the outing.

"Drifting," as it is called, is high-water work. When the drift is running, there is always valuable material running down stream—logs, skiffs, houseboats, barges, etc., etc. Many a man makes good wages catching logs lost from rafts and booms upstream. A skiff, a "dog" to drive into the logs, a hammer or axe, and a stout line are the equipment required. An eddy into which the logs are towed is chosen where the send of the current carries the logs near the still water. It is hard work while it lasts and is exciting because of the chance of being caught, even crushed in the flotsam, but two boys of eighteen years have been known to get a gasoline launch after a season's work, with which the next season was made much more profitable. Towing logs out of the swift, high-water current requires strength and judgment. At the best, the pieces of raft, most valuable finds of all, will occasionally get away, but a handy line run to the bank will swing the heaviest objects ashore.

Fur buying, picking nuts, making willow work, trapping, selling gaudy prints—Biblical subjects, usually—cistern cleaning, are some of the cabin-boat occupations.

One can work his way with photographs or tintypes or both. There are a number of photograph

14 C. B. P.

boats on the Mississippi, but the quality of the work is not high, nor is the field well worked. One should have a fair-sized camera for taking houses and large groups and a small instrument for individuals—plate-holders with 4 x 5 or smaller inserts will serve. Any one willing to tramp from plantation to plantation, haunt the saw mills and levee camps and work steadily can make money on the river—any ordinary river—photographing.

A party of several persons having a good-sized boat will find many a landing where a "show" will draw paying audiences. There are several show boats on the Ohio and Mississippi, one at least, which is towed from town to town by its own steamboat. Music is always in demand, and a "fiddler," banjo player or other musician will often have opportunities to play for such dancing as the wilds alone afford.

Skilled mechanics command high wages along the river, wherever they are needed. Masons, carpenters, painters, blacksmiths, etc., are in demand, especially if they will work steadily and well at moderate prices. Nearly every log camp, sawmill, government works, and levee camp has need of workers. A man who can handle a band saw, or keep a gang of darkies moving is in demand in the Mississippi Bottoms, while the upper rivers offer similar opportunities, each of its own kind. A man able and willing to work need never fear any great time of enforced idleness, although the jack of all trades stands a better show on the average than a master of one, unless that one is sawmilling, logging, cotton raising, or whatever particular operations are going on down the river. A steel man without work in Pittsburg would be an anomaly.

There are, of course, opportunities of permanent work and even fortunes. One could homestead swamp forest land at, say $1.25 or so an acre, clear it and sell it for $30.00 an acre and make the cost of clearing several times over by skillful management of the timber product. Of course, these opportunities grow fewer every year, and are not plenty now.

The customers of a cabin-boat store are usually negroes. Ordinarily cabin-boaters deal almost exclusively with darkies, and are, for this reason and because of certain bad men among them, treated with scorn by those who live behind the levees. But every man is taken at his value and dozens of prosperous Mississippians, Louisianians and other Southerners first came down the river in shanty-boats. I have seen a family on the Tennessee River on its way, bag and baggage, to "Texas" or any other land down stream offering opportunity to a mountaineer from up the French Broad. At Greenville, Miss., I met a painter and his wife who started from Dixon, Ill., with only a cabin-boat and a month's provisions. Merely desiring to travel, they went in the one way open for them— by cabin-boat—and saw the South, paying their way as they went, by his work and her planning.

"We may never go anywhere again," they said, "but we have come this far—more than 2,000 miles —lived better than at home and with far less expenses, less work and more comfort—more real life, than we ever knew at home."

Their boat was 22 feet long and cost less than $30 to build, but it was well build and they made safe landings only.

Of fishing, hunting and trapping, more is said in another chapter. But none of them are to be depended on for more than occasional coins, if any. Hunting

A River Fisherman Raising His Trap.

for market is not encouraged by the Southern States and Tennessee requires a $200 bond, as well as a large license fee from the market shooter. Sale of game is more and more dangerous and will soon be entirely forbidden. Fishing, if followed up for several months, or years, and learned like a trade, is profitable work—till one gets malaria.

On many rivers, pearl and shell fisheries are carried on. Recently, the price paid for button shells had decreased, but money is still to be made dredging the mussel beds for shells and occasionally a lucky strike is made—a pearl is found worth from a few cents up to thousands of dollars. The "slugs" or rough shaped pearl chunks taken from the shells are worth a dollar or so an ounce. The Department of Agriculture has printed several bulletins on this and kindred subjects, which the would-be money maker will do well to look up.

Indeed, if one proposes to go into cabin-boating for the money there is in it, he will do well to make a study of the books which are to be had about the commercial resources of the localities and regions which he intends to visit. It will, at least, do no harm to learn as much as possible about the region to be visited.

Perhaps the most profitable and the most instructive business is peddling. If a man knows how to sell things out of a pack, he will find a ready market for almost anything that is on the market—trinkets, pictures, drygoods,—everything that a peddler ever sold can be sold with a cabin-boat as a basis of operations.

Here is the way a pearler describes his work:

Fresh Water Clams.

I saw in the H-T-T where a man wants to know

how to get fresh water clams without diving for them. The editor gave a very good way, but the way that the editor gave is a very old one and you will get more dead shells than live ones. Here is the way we used to get them at Muscatine, Iowa, the great pearl button center.

First, have a flat bottomed boat 20 feet long; get two pieces of gas pipe $1\frac{1}{4}$ inches in diameter and 12 feet long. Nail pieces of boards to sides of boat 3 feet long, two to each side about one-third of the way from each end, respectively, and have them to stand upright with top end 2 or $2\frac{1}{2}$ ft. higher than top of boat and put hooks on the top of them and hang your gas pipe on, one on each side of the boat. Next, get some rope twine about 3/16 of an inch thick and cut into pieces 5 feet long. Tie one end of the strings on the pieces of gas pipe every 6 inches apart letting the other end hang down. Now all this is easy enough, but here comes the working part of it, especially for a man who never saw it done.

Next, take some fence wire and cut into pieces about 7 inches long; take two pieces at a time and with two pair of pieces twist the middles together like barbed wire is done, only twist tighter, but leave the ends free and untwisted. Now bend them double and twist the double a little to hold them together good, but don't twist the points. Now, bend all four points up like a fish hook. After you have enough of these, tie them on the pieces of cord as the hooks will hang down. Put about four on each cord about 6 inches apart up and down the cord. Now take two pieces of small rope (one rope to each gas pipe) 14 feet long and tie to each end of the gas pipe (drive wood plugs into the end of the gas pipe to tie to and have securely tied). Now take two larger ropes and tie to the middle of smaller ones and long enough to reach bottom and drag hard on the ground. Tie the other ends to boat, one to each side and you are ready for business. Cast one overboard and let your boat float down stream 50 to 75 feet; draw it up and cast the other one over and while you are picking shells off No. 1 No. 2 is catching more.

The live clams under water are open and as the hooks drag over them, they close up catching the hooks as they do so. These two drags will keep you busy pulling clams off your hooks and you aren't bothered with dead shells. If the current is not strong enough to pull the boat and drag, put a buoy on the boat that will catch the water and help pull. After you get a boat load of shells, row to the shore, have a large flat pan over a dugout furnace. Fill it one-half full of water and finish filling with clams; let them boil about ten minutes, take them out with a potato fork and after cool enough you can grab the clams out of the shells as fast as you can pick them up and look for pearls. The shells are also worth $25.00 a ton at the button factories at Muscatine, Iowa. (The boiling does not damage the pearls).

CHAPTER XXIV.

On Making Notes.

A CABIN-BOATER will find a note book of great value, even though incomplete and small. A little trouble will repay the house-boater better in making notes than in any other way. The mere writing down of a fact impresses it on the mind. If one is going down a river, facts about the lower stream put in a note book will remind one of good landings, good hunting, fishing and what not. On the Mississippi, the Ohio, etc., are numerous light houses, all of which are described in a little book issued by the Mississippi River commission, which has them in care. Blank lines in these light books serve admirably for a river index. Suppose one hears that there is good hunting on Big Island. In the light book, at the Big Island light, is written "see page so and so". Page so and so in the note book gives in detail where to land to find the hunting and the name of a cabinboater there, perhaps. So of places to find hickory nuts, to see notable people, to watch out for bad wind landings, to beware of a dangerous man.

As a mere matter of interest, a note book has vast pleasure in it. Take a "Journal" or blank paged day book. Putting in this, from day to day, notes of things seen, done and heard will soon make a volume of unrivaled interest to the maker. There is plenty of time for such work in houseboating. Many river people have these note books, but in most cases the pages are too small—it takes a large hand to attract full detail. A small page cramps the thought. My own preference is a page at least six by eight inches and ten by twelve inches is even better. A journey down the Mississippi from St. Louis to New Orleans will fill hundreds of pages with notes of unexcelled interest and value for the second trip, should one make a second trip.

Of historical places, the Mississippi has countless numbers. From De Soto's crossing down to modern times and any river banks are replete with places of interest—and a note book description of what one sees of them with his own eyes will draw one close to these places and for all time widen his vision of the Nation.

One should use a pen and ink for the notes— pencil marks rub and become illegible. If one has a typewriter it will do no harm to carry it. Thin sheets of paper can be pasted into note books. In this way one can write his notes on the machine and insert them. For letters, the typewriter will also prove of great value.

Making notes serves to pass many an hour when wind bound, or long, dull evenings. A little thought will give one plenty to write about. The trouble on a houseboat is not lack of things to tell, but too many things.

If one is traveling as a matter of education "to see the country", the note book is the most important feature of the trip. What is written down is never forgotten as long as the note book lasts. If one is seeking information on any matter, as timber, cotton industries, birds, trade, manufacturing, speculative opportunities, the note book carefully kept will at least reveal the good opportunities and the bad ones. If one starts from Pittsburg and goes to New Orleans, and gathers notes and statistics found in newspapers, magazines, documents and books, he would have a vast fund of information on which a life's industry might be put—in business, science, or whatever the seeker of information had in mind.

CHAPTER XXV.

Land Hints.

THE cabinboater approaches land from novel conditions. He will live, most of the time, literally upon the water. "Don't get seasick when you go ashore" expresses an odd truth in the cabinboater's life. After days in the wind, the land will seem to fairly dance under his feet.

The cabinboater should never go ashore without taking his bearings by compass and especially when he intends to go hunting. A surveyor with all his instruments, was lost in the "Dark Corner" a few miles above the mouth of the St. Francis beside the Mississippi. Col. Sibley, a famous bear hunter at the mouth of White River, Montgomery chute, told of getting lost on Big Island and wandering for a long time in the cane brake. Col. Sibley then and there invented a rudder which every man and woman approaching a cane brake should know about.

Col. Sibley found it impossible to walk in a straight line. Try as he might, he couldn't do it. But at last he cut a stick of cane as long as he could find. With the butt end of this under his arm, he started. The pole lay out behind him and when he started to walk in a circle the cane held him true to his course—he just couldn't walk in a curve without an increasing pressure on his side warning him.

In the open woods one can always get a straight line by taking three trees in line and picking up a fourth one as the nearest one is passed.

Both these schemes save much compass work—in a cane brake one can not risk dropping the little case by carrying it in his hand. The cane pole rudder keeps him true to his course.

The northerner, used to shrubs and open walking, will find himsef tripping and stumbling in southern woods. He may go on stumbling for months unable to understand how his southern companions keep from falling. The secret lies in the ankle. The southern hunter walks with a limp ankle as each runner slides off his toe, while the northern hunter lifts the vines in the hook of his toe and when he starts forward, the vines hold him back. Not having vines in the north, he never learned to walk as one must walk to avoid them. On the other hand, the stiff brush and dry twigs confuse a southerner when he gets into the north.

Moccasins are unnecessary in the Mississippi Bottoms. One can walk as silently there with heavy soles as with the softest buckskin in the Adirondacks or Canada. The ground is always damp, the twigs always soggy and the leaves always soft and without a rustle. It is the gloom, the tangles of vines and brakes of impenetrable cane that will confuse the mountain hunter there.

Swamps are a thing to be reckoned with. In wet weather keep away from the tupelo gum, which grows in soft, slimy muck into which the unwary may walk unwittingly and sink to his hips before he knows he is in danger.

Here and there in the bottom one will discover holes in the ground—pitfalls to dodge. Trees, surrounded by deposits of silt from the river overflow cause these round holes. The tree dies and decays, leaving a round cavity, sometimes twenty feet deep with water at the bottom. To get into one of them is an experience not to be sought.

If one is hunting and becomes lost towards night, or in the night, very often a hollow tree will offer shelter from wind or storm. A hole scooped out in the soft ground will shelter one from a harsh wind.

The land is divided into two parts, Between the Levees and Behind the Levees. People who live on the banks of the Mississippi take their chances with the floods. Their homes are sometimes two-story buildings, the lower story used ordinarily but the upper one ready for the spring inundation. The voyager will also see homes built on frame work high above the ground. It is worth one's while to see the thousand and one ways of combating the floods. It is presumed that one travels to learn, as much as anything else. People who live along the banks of rivers that rise 65 feet in a spring flood must needs know conditions of which a first-trip cabinboater has no knowledge.

In one sense of the word, shanty-boating is simply finding new lands to travel and a new view-point from which to see the land.

A River Fisherman's Home.

CHAPTER XXVI.

Photographing.

THE cabinboater should surely take a camera, if it is no more than a $5.00 1½ by 2-inch roll film instrument. To record the scenes of a trip down the river, a 4 x 5 plate camera is, all things considered, as good as any. A 3¼ by 4¼ camera will make an album of unrivalled interest. A tripod should be used whenever possible, and the object carefully focused.

In choosing a photograph machine, a simple bellows, plate and film camera is best. It should be of light weight, with a case holding both the camera and plate or film holders and a strap for carrying over the shoulder. A heavy machine tempts one to leave it at home and a complicated one will make many pictures seem unnecessary, although some of the scenes not taken will be mourned for all time afterwards.

The expense of a large instrument overcomes its greatest charm for most people. One hesitates to use a seven-cent 5 x 7 plate on a dull day, although a three- cent 3¼ by 4¼ would be risked—and the result likely to be the pride of months of work. Fortunate is the one who can afford two cameras—a 5 x 7 or 8 x 10 and a 4 x 5 or a 3¼ x 4¼ would then be carried, while a little $5 film camera of smallest size would be kept in the pocket for good measure. The modern lens which comes with complete cameras is fit for beautiful work of the kind that a cabinboater is most likely to do—views, groups and men at their tasks. But they leave considerable room for improvement.

A Bausch & Lomb, Zeiss, Goerz or other high grade lense is a joy almost worth going hungry for. Some artistic photographers pretend to despise the details, but an oak tree without its bark is frequently not an oak at all. Moreover, just as artistic landscapes can be made with a lens showing the furthest reaching vine tendril, as with one that makes a tree's fluffed branches a mere splash of flat shade. Another reason for the costly lens is the fact that most cabinboat pictures are likely to be made from an unstable craft, where great speed is necessary.

It is worth while at the beginning of a trip, to make up one's mind what sort of pictures are desired most. Few novices are satisfied with their subjects because they take too many pictures of no use whatever, not even to the memory. Let every one get in mind certain lines of subjects and make their pictures close to that line. This will result in series of pictures.

A cabinboater will have many broad groups to choose from. If he is interested particularly in people, let him make character photographs of men at their labors, women at their gossip and children at their play. The river offers countless views—but each picture should tell something about the stream—how it wears the rock, or wears away the bank, how it piles up the drift and spreads out the sand, how it plunges down the shoals and swirls gently in the eddy. If one watches for his opportunity, he can get in fifty well chosen photographs what a thousand plates snapped without thought would fail to show. There are few men who kill all kinds of game with equal pleasure—the bird hunter is at variance with the man who hunts deer. The camera man must make up his mind to choose his own game, hunt it with avidity and ceaseless, loving care. If one day his enthusiasm is for huge trees, the next for ragged children, the third for quaint houses, the fourth for artistic groups of cattle and people—he must expect sooner or later to arrive at the feeling of disappointment felt by many a sportsman who, after testing the pleasures of all the fun seeking tarpon to shooting at grizzly bears, suddenly finds himself a mere tyro in all sports, instead of the honored expert of a few. The cabinboater can not photograph everything worth having, but he can get every phase of the river, he can picture every river type, he can gather views of homes and trails, or anything else he wishes, but everything should be in series. The lone plate, without connection or comparison, is sometimes a wasted effort. The most cherished picture is one that stands above a hundred, or a thousand of its kind.

The cabinboater should develop his pictures as he goes along. Prepared chemicals are easiest to get along with under such circumstances, but preparation for the minor difficulties due to heat and the change of water should be prepared for. A filtering jug, a large tub for washing plates, if the river water is not clear and ordinary plate and paper materials should be provided. But the trays that have extra high sides, to prevent the waves from a passing steamer or wind, sloping the developer, are worth while. Develop out papers are likely to prove most satisfactory.

A dark room is not necessary. It would be small and uncomfortable at best, unless one fitted a whole cabin with light-tight windows, doors and walls. With the chemicals dissolved and ready for instant use in bottles—carefully labeled—a great deal of work can be done on the kitchen table between nightfall and bed time.

15 C. B. P.

Ice is to be had in practically all southern river towns.

In recent years, the developing tank has been introduced; one puts a dozen plates into a tank, pours in the developer, and lets it stand an hour, more or less. Then fixer is poured in, and the plates are done, without more worry.

The printing papers are easily manipulated, and if one has a carbide gas light, just an ordinary bicycle lamp or motorcycle lamp, prints may be made rapidly and easily, developing being done in the boat, while prints are made on the bow or stern deck.

Of all records of a trip, none is more interesting than that made by frequently exposures of the camera—this cannot be too much insisted upon, and a good camera is never wasted, if one uses it. One never meets a traveler who has been far who does not regret not having even a cheap photographing outfit with him, to take the pictures he would best enjoy recalling.

CHAPTER XXVII.

GAME AND HUNTING.

THE good sportsman, seeking pleasure, and novel experiences, will find them in his houseboat journeys. For rivers without serious obstacles to flatboat navigation, the ideal camp for hunters is the cabinboat. One moves with it from locality to locality and whatever may be the conditions of the land roundabout, the cabinboat is dry, warm and comfortable. In a land of swamps, where camping places are far between and where the tents must often have board floors, the cabinboat is a joy.

It would be futile to attempt to give a full treatise on hunting from a cabinboat, but it is worth while giving a few special hints and random observations, in order that the cabinboater may equip himself for his sport.

Shooting wild fowl will be the cabinboater's ordinary sport on most streams. He should have a gun for ducks and other birds. He will find squirrels and wild geese, coons and opossums, sometimes wild turkey and deer along most cabinboat streams.

The cabinboater should go equipped for night hunting—not "jacking" but with a head light. Shooting deer, ducks, geese, etc., at night is frowned upon by many states and by all sportsmen, but the raccoon and opossum hunting is a real sport, whether done with dogs or by fire alone. A good headlight is an acetylene lamp, fitted to wear on the head. It should not be heavy. One finds the Mississippi bottom hunters us-

Duck Hunters and Their Retrievers.

ing a two-torch kerosene headlight, which does good work and costs only half a dollar. But this light often leaks around the burners and a hunter must carry a chunk of soap to stop up the cracks. Also, the provident hunter carries a bottle of oil in his pocket lest the oil burn out

The best sort of night for raccoon and opossum hunting is cloudy, so one will not mistake stars for eyes, and quiet, warm and balmy. The animals are usually found around nut (pecan, etc.) trees, grape vines, persimmon trees, and along the edges of bayous. They are fattest in the fall and winter.

In many places along the Mississippi one will find bear, deer, panther, wild cats, wild turkeys, etc., etc. In the overflow of springs, these animals are driven to the high lands, where one will find them, gaunt, water-tamed and pitiful in the extreme.

Huge swamp rabbits are everywhere in the bottoms. Hunting them is great sport, requiring good marksmanship for they are swift runners. Where there are nuts, one will find foxes and gray or black squirrels.

Wild turkeys are plentiful in certain sections, but to get them requires much skill. Turkey calls are essential as a rule.

One will do much of his hunting in a row boat, paddling up and down bayous and along swamp rivers. In the overflow, one can hunt in no other way. Perhaps as thrilling an experience as the cabin-boater will have is going back into a wilderness in his boat and perhaps coming upon a bear in the water or on a log. Col. Sibley tells of hunting a wounded bear in a little dugout canoe. The bear got a claw on the side of the boat and upset it, but Sibley fought it out with his knife and the bear sank in ten feet of water. Col. Sibley was unable to find the place when he had gotten a boat hook, so never recovered the animal.

A tracking snow sometimes comes to the swamps of Arkansas and then one can find coon trees and even panther and bear dens. The swamp hunter of Arkansas crawls through the cane and finds the bears in a hibernating coma and kills them. One old hunter, Patterson, famous up the St. Francis, was going home one night when his dogs were attacked by a panther— perhaps it was the other way. The row invited Patterson and he went in, knife in hand. By feeling the texture of the hair he was able to locate the panther and stabbed repeatedly. In the morning, the first road follower found the man in alcoholic sleep, with three dead panthers for pillow and foot rests.

Let it not be forgotten that one will get lost in an Arkansas swamp quicker than anywhere else in North America. Even if one is in a boat, he must exercise every caution in venturing out of sight of his cabinboat. The mariner at sea does not have more use for a compass than a hunter in the overflow, or in the brakes.

When the snow is on the ground, the cabinboater will have a fine opportunity to find bee trees and load up with a hundred or so gallons of wax and honey. Around bee trees are always to be found the dead insects, which are conspicuous in the snow. On warm days or in the summer the hum of the bees around a bee tree can be heard a long distance. On a warm winter day, the insects come out of the tree and fairly roar, apparently engaged in taking the kink out of their stiffened muscles.

The duck and geese hunters use decoys to advantage on the Mississippi. There are many points and bars where these birds come so often as not to require decoys, although a good call and a few decoys can be used to advantage. There are certain localities where ducks stop for several weeks, perhaps for all winter. Here the gunning is excellent. A locality full of old river lakes, ponds and sloughs is likely to be such a locality and the sportsman will do well to inquire along for such places. They are often at a distance from towns and little frequented by gunners.

The first flight of birds out of the North or from the South is considered best by the valley hunters. That is, they kill more game in these flights. A foggy day will sometimes bring the game flocking down upon a hunter in a blind. But these are not the great joy of the cabinboating sportsman. He doesn't want a barrel of ducks but instead, meals of ducks scattered along during the whole period of his journey.

Some special dishes are to be bagged by the cabinboater, which are not thought of at other times. Muskrats, well parboiled with soda, breasts of cranes and gulls, etc., etc., are a few of the game heads one might try to advantage. In the South, robins are regarded as game, being found in unimaginable flocks there. Also it will give a cabinboater many meals if he will shoot blackbirds and bake them in a pie. The blackbirds can be killed around corn cribs and at their roosts at sundown. Few birds have a better flavor.

One's choice of weapons depends on the chooser to a great extent Small game will be the rule. A 12 or 16 gauge shotgun, using chilled shot, will probably give one more all around satisfaction than any other weapon. If one wants a weapon for fun, doubtless a .22 caliber rifle, shooting a Winchester rifle cartridge will give more than any other fire arm. It is fine

Seineing Fish For Market in the South.

Market Fishermen and Their Catch.

for squirrels, ducks, rabbits, etc., etc. For geese, wild
turkeys and heavier game, a .30-30, .32-40, .38-55, etc.,
etc., are as good as any at long range.

A word of caution in regard to hunting must be
given. Every state has game laws, more or less strictly
enforced. Arkansas forbids non-residents hunting,
but this law is seldom enforced against men who bear
themselves in a becoming manner. The law was de-
signed to discourage market hunters and game hogs,
which it has done. Where game is not plenty, local
hunters are sometimes jealous of visitors, but due
regard for local feelings and decent regard of conditions, will give one opportunity to keep small game
upon the table almost anywhere. The cabinboater
will get his best sport with small game.

In recent years, the game laws have closed down
hard. The game has grown so scarce everywhere,
and has disappeared in so many places that the legis-
latures have made drastic efforts to prevent unnecessary and destructive killing. Wherever one goes now,
the game protector is on his trail and watching him
every day, especially if he is a stranger and seems to
have plenty of money. Some towns seem to try to
support themselves by fining outsiders, while letting
their own people waste and destroy without sense and
without excuse. The non-resident is hunted from
place to place wherever he goes.

Of all the things in hunting, perhaps none is quite
so exasperating as the non-resident license law. The
states play favorites, their own people against all
comers, and every out-door man knows with what
gross favoritism game laws are often administered.
In spite of the United States Constitution, petty of-
ficials make the hunting laws a vehicle of extortion
by which to mulct "foreigners" of fines merely be-

cause they have fire arms on their persons—the New York pistol toting law, for example, and the fact that if a man without a hunting license carries a gun in or out of season is made sufficient excuse to hale him into court and fine him. Instead of growing better, the game laws and their enforcement are more and more bringing discomfort for ordinary gun users and bearers.

Of course, the excuse is that some men are game hogs, killing more than their share, and any one who kills game without excuse is simply adding to the local bitterness against strangers. It is up to every man to do his best to give no cause for complaint in the matter of hunting and fishing.

CHAPTER XXVIII.

TRAPS AND TRAPPING.

A GREAT deal of interesting experience and some little profit may be had by taking advantage of opportunities to catch fur bearers which cabin-boating gives almost anywhere. On the Mississippi River and its tributaries one will find a few steel traps, some snare wire and a scent bait or two of much value.

Coons, opossums, mink, skunks, foxes, otter, wild cats—in fact most fur bearers are to be found along the various streams. Uncle Charlie Robertson, a river man, when timber-looking becomes too monotonous, goes far up the Missouri, and traps down, seeking especially the little lakes remote from ordinary hunters' and trappers' grounds. On a trip of three or four months, he sometimes takes a thousand or fifteen hundred pieces, making good wages. Only an expert should dream of doing this, however.

The ordinary man, trapping for fun (cruel as it is) must expect to catch very little, or in proportion to his experience and efforts. By watching the banks, places where coon and opossum come down to drink are to be found and at the water's edge, a white pearl button or white feather or piece of meat, may lure the animal's paw into the trap.

One may discover otter slides, at the foot of which a trap may get a captive. Here and there, when one learns that wildcats are plenty, these creatures can be taken with meat bait, or by traps at the mouth of their dens.

Along the Mississippi, the trapper will find a ready sale for coon and 'possum carcasses at 25 cents each, the negroes being glad to get them at that price. If one catches fur, it will pay to treat it carefully. The ordinary way of stretching coon and 'possum skins on pieces of cane, slits being cut along both sides of the pelt and then the sticks threaded through the slits and spread apart by cross pieces, is very wasteful. A much more economical way would be to have thin boards cleated together so as to make a perfectly flat surface large enough to hold the skin inside down. On this the skin is carefully stretched and tacked down. The hair is combed with a coarse comb and tangles straightened out. Skins treated that way bring a fourth more than ordinary, careless stretching, and sun-and-rain exposure.

No. 1 steel traps, with the spring under the pan are best for trapping muskrats, mink, etc. Large sizes are necessary for large game.

There is an unwritten law that one's trapping land shall not be invaded by another, nor shall another man's traps be interfered with. There are also state laws in regard to fur-bearing animals which should be looked up by the would-be trapper.

If one traps at all, he will do well to learn from local trappers the usual method followed, and then do something different. For instance, the water set is used almost exclusively in the swamps of Arkansas, but there are long seasons in which coons and 'possums do not come to the bayous and rivers. There can be no question but what land sets at feeding grounds could surprise the coons, sometimes even the wise old fellows, who know every water set trick from pieces of pearl to imitation crawfish holes in the bank.

Also, in trapping as in hunting and fishing, one must watch out for the local laws and ordinances. Violations are made very expensive these days, and before setting out one's traps in a strange state, it would be best to study the lay of the land for a day or two, and find out the temper and the habits of the local people. This might save a good deal of money.

CHAPTER XXIX.

Fish and Fishing.

THE cabin-boater will have opportunity for about all kinds of inland fishing there is, if he travels in his floating home upon the proper streams.

The Mississippi watershed is probably the best black bass region in the world. Most of the rivers and many of the lakes are full of game fish. If one is out for fishing sport he will do well to make inquiries of the state game and fish wardens, as to what is to be expected in certain streams and fit out accordingly. One should be able to at least keep himself supplied with fish food on a cabin-boat journey. Very often a line with a hook and sinker and bait dropped over the side of a boat will give as many fish as are wanted. Of course much depends on the season.

Where bass are to be had, take bass tackle. Within three or four years (1903) Librarian Johnson (Cossitt Library, Memphis) introduced flies and the fly rod to the St. Francis River, and while the natives stood watching the sight, dubious and polite, he caught more than they could with all the cane poles. One will find countless streams where he can introduce new and effective methods of fishing for fun. But he should not despise local sports, or methods. Take, for instance, jugging for big catfish on the Mississippi crossings.

Hooks three or four inches long are baited with chunks of pork, liver, half of rabbits, squirrels or anything of the kind. These are tied at the ends of lines six or eight feet long and at the upper end a wooden block, corked jug, or other float is fastened. Ten or twenty of these lines are set afloat at the head of a shoal crossing and started down with the current. The bait drifts down to a catfish which proceeds to make the jug dance or dip the little flags on the blocks. The fishermen, floating along in their skiffs, race from jug to jug, untangling those that get hung on snags and lifting out 150-pound cats on occasions.

For table fish, one may sometimes find it expedient to set a trot or jump line. These lines are sometimes hundreds of feet long, with a hook on 9 or 12-inch staging every six feet or so. Baited with bits of meat, stiff boiled dough, mingled with lint or cotton, or with sundry other baits, they are very effective and some river fishermen make their living fishing these in season.

The lines are set along the river reefs, if possible just under the crest of the flowing sand. The fish and eels gather along the edge of the reefs, and as their food is washed down the slope, pick it from the face of the sand wave. If the line baits are well placed, nearly every hook will frequently catch its victim, in a night. Of course, a short trot line will serve to keep one boat supplied with fish, if they are biting. A ten-pound blue cat or two will make a meal for quite a boat load.

The old rivers, lakes and ponds back from the main river are great fishing places and cabin-boat parties should try them for game fish, perch, black bass, etc., etc. Of course, in the upper rivers, one will do well to run up some of the little creeks to see what they have to offer. One will often find splendid fishing in these little streams, especially if they do not happen to have been netted.

Below Knoxville, Tennessee, on the Tennessee River, graining or spearing huge carp, or buffalo and catfish is practiced by firelight by the residents along the river. Standing in the bow of a narrow canoe, throwing a spear with line attached, cannot fail to be a sport attractive to many a roamer of flowing waters.

Of netting, only a few hints can be given. In the lakes, nets, seines and pounds are used. The seines are sometimes hundreds of feet long and are drawn to the banks with windlass or even teams of horses.

During the overflow nets are run through the woods hundreds of yards, the fish following the twine fences to pockets from which they are lifted by the fishermen.

In the main river, hoop, or dyke nets are set in the places where the fish pass certain points and go through certain channels. The fisherman must know the fish swimways as the trappers know fur-bearers' runways. Some men can never learn this, while others, like Seabold down Atchafayala, clears his $50 a week during the season.

Market fishing along the Mississippi is a profitable business, steady workers getting as high as a thousand dollars a year. The equipments can be home made. Hook nets cost about $6.00 apiece and some seines, several hundred dollars. I saw a fisherman at Lake Province sell $79.00 worth of fish one afternoon on the streets of that town. He paid the state for the exclusive privilege of fishing the old river lake at that town.

The Mississippi reaching from speckled trout to tarpon and alligator and gar waters, offers a thousand

16 C. B. P.

Fish Net Reel, Mississippi River.

Cabin of a Lake Providence, La., Fisherman, Showing the Net Reel.

varieties of fishing. In the bayous of Louisiana the trot lines are made of wire clothes line, because alligator gar bite the cotton lines in two. Throughout the length of the river, tar-flecked clothes are the sign of the fishermen, for nets and lines must be tarred to save them from the tepid waters.

The cabin-boater should by all means do a little fishing now and then. A line, a chunk of lead and some hooks will nearly always supply the table with fish in Mississippi basin waters and rod and reel sport is to be had from end to end of the rivers or adjacent ponds.

Of course, there is special preparation needed for a successful fishing campaign, and people who expect to pay expenses anywhere by fishing for market are very likely to get into trouble financially.

As in hunting laws, fishing laws are found loaded for the fisherman in many states, and there are game wardens who use the laws with utmost rigor against the stranger and the friendless—even as other laws are used.

CHAPTER XXX.

Amusements — Books.

ON a prolonged cabin-boat journey provision must be made for preventing time hanging heavily on one's hands, otherwise a rainy day may take away the keen pleasure of the trip.

Many a cabin-boater learns to play the banjo, violin, accordeon or other instrument on odd days. The flowing water is an inspiration and mere idleness is more difficult on a cabin-boat than anywhere else in the world.

It is not advisable to play poker with one's cabin-boat neighbors, for some of them read the backs of their cards far more readily than amateurs read their faces. Nevertheless, a pack of cards will while away an hour or two in as useless a way as one could desire. A more stimulating pleasure is to be had at checkers, backgammon or chess and it is worth while to take along a checker player's book, learn the number, the leading games, etc.

A rainy or a windy day is a good time to make changes in the boat—put in a new partition, fit a trap door in the floor, fix a cupboard, add a closet to the space under the stern or bow decks, or otherwise improve a boat's appearance.

A heavy day is often a good day for mending, making extra dishes of food, cleaning up, washing clothes, repairing shoes, etc., etc.

The river fisherman usually keeps a ball of twine on hand so that he can start a net when a bad day comes. The hunter will overhaul his gun or rifle and perhaps load a cartridge or two with a special charge—ammunition is usually purchased ready loaded. A junker will sort his brass, light from heavy, and examine his odds and ends to see if some valuable, old-fashioned trinket has not crept into his cargo. The trapper will comb the fur of his catch, giving it a neater, more valuable appearance. The tripper of experience will overhaul his ropes and see that ends do not need winding with twine, or a chafed place cut away.

Those who keep diaries should go back over their notes and add omitted items and write for the day the thousand things that spring to the mind.

The photographer may draw down the wooden slides of the kitchen windows, or tack over them some thick, opaque material and make prints of plates and films by lamplight—daylight printing on a clouded day is the most unsatisfactory task in photographing.

A few books, well chosen, are a joy of life in a cabin-boat. A volume or two of bound magazines is sure to contain satisfactory reading for any mood. If one chooses a magazine of travel, especially of American travel, the chances are, something interesting and valuable will be found in it about one's own river. It is a first-class plan to take special pains to get books treating of the region through which one is traveling. The voyager on the Holston crosses every trail Daniel Boone followed to Kentucky, and the Holston River is a long line of historical places. Nowhere in the country will one see so many mounds as when floating down the Tennessee. And on the Tennessee, from end to end, the traveler passes places famous in world history—Chattanooga and Shiloh, for instance.

It is not necessary to make a study of the region —though this has charms indescribable. A map of the river, a state history or two and odds and ends of literature relating to the particular region in which one is, adds vastly to the enjoyment of a journey down the stream. Unfortunately, few rivers have good books written about them. But in three or four books the cabin-boater will be able to get the main features of the Ohio, Mississippi, Tennessee or other rivers.

In selecting light reading for a journey, the cabin-boater will be guided chiefly by taste, but it should not be forgotten that every section of the country has its own special fiction and that nowhere can a reader get so much enjoyment from a good book as in the land of which it treats. John Fox's books are best loved by ones who have seen Kentuckians and know the mountain people of whom it tells. Cable's Creoles are best appreciated when one is in Louisiana. The cabin-boater in Carolina, Georgia or Alabama Rivers will rejoice in every one of Joel Chandler Harris' Uncle Remus stories. It is worth while to confine one's self exclusively to typical local literature when he goes afloat in a cabin-boat.

But in choosing books, let them be standard works. Nowhere do the errors of poor observers or false prophets stand out so glaringly as in their books when read "on the spot." If one does not choose well, the books selected will fail to relieve the tedium which they should relieve. In impatience, the books will be tossed aside, and the cabin-boater will pace the floor, wondering vainly what to do.

One whose tastes run to certain subjects, will do well to carry his favorites along. The nature student, especially, cannot fail to find himself gratified by new observations when afloat. He should prepare for birds, beasts, trees, flowers, mosses, or whatever his line may be. To no one does the mocking bird sing so beautifully or the huge trees seem so majestic, or the geological formations appear so attractive as to the man in a cabin-boat.

Cabin-boating accentuates a man's good features and brings up and satisfies his latent desires. It is worth while passing a hint in regard to companions. If one goes alone on his cabin-boat, he has everything his own way. One companion adds company and takes away considerable freedom of movement. Two companions may lead to a cabin-boat full of dissensions. One gets very close to the nature of comrades afloat. A certain liking for roughing it must be in the heart of the cabin-boater, else traveling with the current proves distasteful. The lone man will often find a dog most companionable, but it is nothing to a man's credit if he cannot get along with most kinds of people. Still, it is worth while exercising a good deal of discretion when taking to cabin-boating for a month or months.

A special warning against "picking up" companions on a river should be given. River tramps and thieves wander up and down cabin-boat streams, seeking an opportunity to steal a skiff or house-boat. They seek to ingratiate themselves into the good graces of a man, or party, afloat, and at the first opportunity make way with all that they can. They even do murder, if it seems worth while. The appearance of a cabin-boat outfit bespeaks the occupants as a rule. One will find many a kindly heart among river "shanty-boaters" and long before one meets a man, the cabin-boater's reputation can be learned if one listens carefully to the gossip of casual river acquaintances—and he must travel fast to outrun his own fame, it may be added.

It is said down the Mississippi that there is more music than most people can hear. Certain it is that there are some fine musicians who play on the river shanty-boats. There is no place where music sounds sweeter, and even the French harp—the humble mouth organ—is there a worthy instrument, as well as violin, guitar and banjo. The talking machine with plenty of records is a solace for gloomy days and long evenings. One could do much worse than carry a good supply of music with him. The river music helps one understand the river better than ever—especially down Old Mississip'.

CHAPTER XXXI.

Trapper's Canoe.

CUT a small tree the length you wish your boat, hew it down to two inches wide and one and one-half inches thick, with both ends curved up, say six inches. This will make the keel and curve in each end. This will make the boat with a spoon-shaped bottom, which is a good thing, for it sits on the water like a duck. Now put in between two studdings nailed together to keep it straight, put in the shade and let it dry. Then get all the barrel hoops you can, rasp them down with a horse rasp, because the staves are thicker on one end than the other, screw them on the keel. Ours is four inches from center to center of the staves, the closer the better. Get two soft wood sidings, rip two pieces off each siding two inches wide, put one on the inside of the staves, spring it out until it will be 40 inches across the center, put the other strip on the outside of the staves. Nail through the two strips and the barrel staves with $1\frac{1}{4}$ and $1\frac{1}{2}$-inch clinch nails, according to thickness of strips and staves. Do the same on the other side and see that you get the staves even. Now screw or nail the strips to the end of the piece standing in end of keel, spring the strips so that they will be two feet apart, about $2\frac{1}{2}$ feet from end of boat, put in some $\frac{1}{2}$-inch boards in the $2\frac{1}{2}$-foot space from end and nail it good.

Ours is twelve feet long and one foot deep from keel to top of strips in center. Put in two one-foot wide boards, tapering on one side of ribs or staves.

Now you are ready to put on the canvas. I have sent to a supply house for our canvas of the 20-ounce kind, 60 inches wide, and cost about 60 cents a yard. Stretch canvas over the ends where you boarded the end. Now turn the boat upside down, put a strip of board outside the canvas on the keel, and a few strips on each side to protect the canvas from rocks and snags. Apply a coat of hot linseed oil, when dry you can paint it if you like. Put oarlocks between strips. We got ¾-inch wagon box iron on the outside and inside of the top strips to strengthen them. The boat will cost about $5.00. I do not know just exactly how heavy it is.

MAINE CANOES AND THEIR EQUIPMENT.

The canoe is used extensively in Maine. It is especially adapted to long trips on rivers where there are many portages, as it weighs about eighty-five pounds and one man can carry it. The sportsman often makes a canoe trip of 200 miles in a comparatively short time.

One should be careful when canoeing as the canoe is very easily upset. The stem or stern should be kept in the wind and in rough water.

This craft can be built by any person skilled in the use of tools, but to make a good one, a form on which to build it is most desirable, although not necessary. The cost of building a form is almost as much as the cost of building the canoe, therefore many prefer to pay $30.00 for a conoe all ready for use.

The canvas used in making one of these canoes is eight oz. and is all in one piece without seams. All wood for its construction should be cedar, except that for the thwarts and stems. These parts are made of a tough stiff wood—white oak, hard maple or ash.

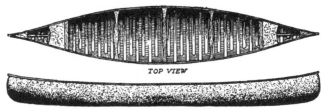

TOP VIEW

SIDE. VIEW

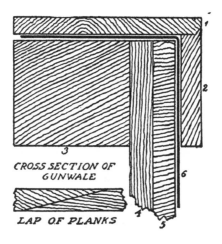

CROSS SECTION OF
GUNWALE

LAP OF PLANKS

The following dimensions may prove helpful to the prospective builder. The length of the canoe is 18 feet, the width at the middle is 34 inches. The depth in the middle is 14 inches and in the bow and stern 17 inches. The wedge is 6 inches long and 1 inch thick. At the width end it is 4 inches and tapers to a point. The gunwales are 1 inch by ⅝ inch; the rails 1 inch by ¼ inch. The cedar planking is 3-16 inch thick; the ribs, also of cedar are ¼ inch thick. These ribs are 2 inches wide in the center, while at each end they are 1½ inches. They are placed about 2 inches apart, except in the end, where the distance between them is 3 or 4 inches. The short ribs are about 1 inch wide and ¼ inch thick, and are placed between the long ribs. They do not extend to the gunwales in this canoe.

In the accompanying drawings the top view shows the long ribs that go from one rail or gunwale to the other. There are thwarts from rail to rail to stiffen the canoe. The seat is a piece of canvas stretched from gunwale to gunwale with the front edge fastened to a thwart. There are wedges in the bow and stern to which the gunwales are nailed.

This small diagram shows how the ribs, planking, canvas, top rail, gunwale and side rail are put together; (1) top rail; (2) side rail; (3) gunwale; (4) ribs; (5) planking; (6) canvas.

The other small diagram shows how the wedge is placed.

(1-1) shows gunwales, side and top rails, one on each side of the wedge and stern.

(2) Shows stern. The ends of the planking are fastened to the stern and it comes down inside

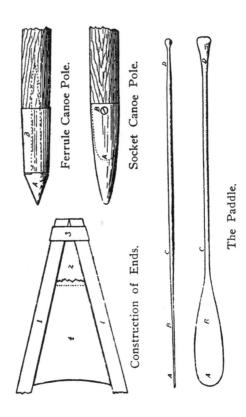

Ferrule Canoe Pole.

Socket Canoe Pole.

Construction of Ends.

The Paddle.

the canoe on top of the ribs in the ends. (See top
view.) The stem extends back under the first thwart
in each end.

(3) Shows metal band which passes around 1-1
to hold them together solidly.

(4) Shows the wedge, the point of which runs
over and covers the top of the stem (2).

The choice of paddles and a pole is important for
a well equipped canoe. The paddles should be large
enough to get a good hold in the water, and long
enough that one can stand while canoeing down swift
water and steer clear of the rocks ahead.

The wood used for the paddles should be sea-
soned, hard maple.

The blade is 8½ inches at the widest part, ½
inch thick at the center at (A) and 5-16 inch thick at
(B). The paddle is about 1¼ inch thick where the
handle and blade join. The handle at (C) is 1⅜
inch by 1⅛ inch, from the front to the back of the
paddle. The handle grows thinner and wider at (D)
and ends with a knob, about 1⅛ inch in diameter,
rounded for the hand to grasp.

This paddle will have quite a spring at (B) if
correctly made. If one prefers a stiff paddle, the
spring is overcome by making it thicker at (B). The
thickness at (A) prevents the paddle from splitting
when it hits rocks.

The pole which is used when canoeing up swift
water, is made of spruce, which is free from knots.
When finished this pole should be about 11 feet long
and should taper evenly from 1¼ inch at the top to
1¼ inch at the end. There are two kinds of poles,
the pike and ferrule, and the socket pike.

In the pike and ferrule pole (B) is the ring which
is a trifle smaller than the pole, and is driven over the

end of it to prevent the pole splitting when the pike (A) is driven into the pole. The pike should be driven into the shoulders as shown by the dotted lines in the illustration.

The socket pike pole is sharpened at the end and driven into the socket to the bottom (A). The pike is solid from (A) to the point. A hole is made in the socket, and after the pole has been driven in, a screw (B) is screwed through the socket into the pole to prevent the pole from coming out of the socket.

While details of construction are not fully given in this description, the writer desires this article to be helpful both to those interested in canoeing and to the amateur builder of canoes.

Building a Boat.

As I have been asked, I will try to give my way of building a boat on a cheap plan and simple to build. I have just made one for this winter's trapping. Get six pieces, 1 x 12, 16 feet long and clear of knots and cracks; four 1 x 4, sixteen feet; one piece 3 x 10, six feet long, five pounds eight penny cut casing nails, one pound four penny wire nails and one gallon coal tar will add greatly to the life of the boat.

Pick the two best planks you have and lay them on the benches, one on the other, and see that the edges are together even. Now mark 5 feet from the end and 7 inches from the bottom edge at end, 4½ feet from the other end and 4 inches from the bottom edge at end. Strike a line and rip off like No. 1.

Now cut the ends of your 3 x 10; the back end should be 24 inches on top and 20 inches at bottom and front end 22 at top and 18 at bottom; when cut it will be like No. 2.

Now place sides on the ground and nail in the ends. I tie a rope around the ends and twist it with a stick to keep the nails from drawing out until some

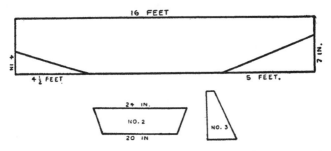

of the bottom is nailed on. Now spread sides as much as you can in the middle and tack a strip across to hold open. You now have your boat in the right shape.

Take a plane or drawing knife and draw off edges of the sides to make the bottom fit smooth. Begin at either end and put the bottom on crosswise, cut the pieces long enough to saw off all around after the bottom is on. Now take three of the 1 x 4 strips, cut them the length of boat on inside; nail on straight through the center on inside and divide the difference between the center and the side of boat; for the others, drive 4-penny nails from the outside and clinch on inside.

Now turn your boat over and cut 8 knees like No. 3.

Take pains to nail them opposite one another. Now cut four pieces out of the 1 x 4 the length of the width of the inside of boat at the knees; saw a notch out of the ends so as to come down straddle of knees and against the strips running lengthwise. This

17 C. B. P.

braces the boat and adds greatly to the strength of it. I have heard men say that they would not have a boat with the bottom crosswise. It makes the best of all. There is no strain on the nails and it will not split the lumber like one when you have to bend it to give it the shape. A man can take pains and build a nice-looking boat on this plan and can put as much finish to it as he wishes.

This boat can be made in any size a man wants, and is strong and easy to run. I make a good many boats and some one is forever wanting them, and I generally sell and make me another one. The tar ought to well boiled and put on like paint. It makes a boat last as long again.

Boat or Skiff Pattern.

I will try to give a boat or skiff pattern, which I have been using and building for 15 years, and it gives better satisfaction than any other model for my use. The way I build this skiff is first to get a 4 x 4 for the front piece or stem, and trim as shown in cut. Next cut your sides and nail both to stem, mark both sides for center frame and nail one side to frame in

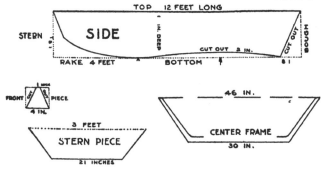

proper place. Then take a good, stout rope and put around the sides back of center frame, well toward the back end. Now take a stick and twist the rope until the other end fits the frame, nail good and put small board across the bottom to hold in place.

Then put other frames and stern piece on; the stern should have more flats than the center. For my use I use just one frame in the center and put bottom on crosswise, but it makes some easier running to put in a frame every 2½ or 3 feet and put bottom lengthwise. I use the lightest lumber I can get for my boats and only one-half to three-fourths inch thick.

ICE-BOATS.

Ice-boats are a very nice thing for a trapper who traps on a large lake. When it is frozen over he can sail around the lake in no time.

A good size for a small boat would be 8 x 11 feet, or 10 x 14 feet. My kind is 8½ x 11½ feet. There are two different makes, the Madison and the Hudson River. The Hudson River is a racing boat. The Madison is also a good boat and I like it better because it has a large cockpit. My make is the Madison.

Madison Ice Boat.

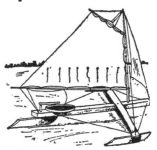
Hudson River Ice Boat.

Now I suppose that none of you trappers know what a cockpit is. It is the seat of the boat and is in the back part of the boat. The different parts of the boat are runner, plank, cockpit, mast, boom, gaff, gib-boom, stave, bridge, sails and runners.

CHAPTER XXXII.

A CABIN-BOAT COON HUNT.

IN November, 1897, the writer and three friends, John Parks, Fred Wyant and Charles Graves, decided upon a trip down the Mississippi River on a coon-hunting and fur-buying expedition, and forthwith cast about for a good and staunch craft in which to sail. After a few busy days spent along the river front of St. Louis, Mo., we found one to our liking and purchased it, together with a skiff, for $225. It was a very nice boat, 9 feet wide and 36 feet long, housed over and containing three cozy rooms and an engine room with a pilot house above. It was fitted with a stern wheel driven by a six-horse gasoline engine and chain gear. We at once gave it a coat of paint, of which it was sadly in need, and named it "Good Cheer." We put in a supply of eatables, drinkables, etc., and elected our officers for the trip as follows: Parks, being a mechanical genius, was given the post of engineer; Wyant, as captain; Graves was installed as chef and the writer as pilot. So there we were, for all the world like the Moorish army, all officers and no men.

On the morning of November 10, we weighed anchor and turned our bows down stream with our flag, a coon skin, flying to the breeze. By the captain's orders she was held to her course until the middle of the afternoon, when we tied up on the Illinois side, a few miles above Chester. That night we had our first hunt. After supper we unchained the dogs, of which we had nine; an old bull bitch and her eight pups, all of one litter by a shepherd dog and all the property of our chef, Graves. We clambered up the bank and started the dogs.

I think a word or two about the training of those dogs will not come amiss. Here, Graves, let me say, was a fisherman, and always made it a business to have a good coon dog or two. A friend gave him this bitch and he used to take her out with a hound he had and he said that he soon noticed that she had a good nose. He said that he had always wanted a coon dog that would run still and not tongue, so he bred her to a shepherd dog, who was a good coon dog himself, and trained the pups with the hound, and the writer will say that he has seen many coon dogs, but none to equal those eight pups (5 dogs and 3 bitches). They were the best rangers I ever saw; would work from a half mile to a mile and a half ahead and when they treed, would stay there until some one came, and any one of them would put the fixing to a coon in short order.

We started the dogs soon after dark and in less than twenty minutes they treed. We hurried there, flashed the bullseye and saw we had two on a small, bushy willow about twenty feet tall. Parks did the monkey act and shook them out. The dogs killed them and left and we soon heard them again. This time it was an opossum—an old bouncer. A long wait and at 10 o'clock we heard them again, but away off. We went there and found them at a hollow log that lay on the ground. As we had no ax with us, we plugged the hole and started back to the boat to turn in. On our way back we got one, the dogs getting him on the ground. We arrived at the boat and turned in for the night.

After breakfast Wyant, Parks and I took our

guns, an ax and the dogs and went to the hollow log. With considerable work and some swearing by Wyant (the log was a sycamore), at which Parks and I laughed, we finally got a hole cut and began killing coons. We got eight from the log, all one family, by the size and the looks, which made us eleven coon and one opossum for the first night's work. On our second night we split into two parties, Wyant and I taking four dogs and the skiff and going to the Missouri side. The others got in at midnight with 5 coon and 2 opossum, while Wyant and I were two hours later with 3 coon, 3 opossum, 1 skunk, 1 mink. We went down the stream a few miles the next day and worked both sides two nights, getting 20 coon, 16 opossum and 3 skunk. We landed at Cairo on December 10, where we made our first shipment of fur: .380 coon, 416 opossum, 26 skunk and 9 mink, which with 50 green pelts on hand, made us 881 pelts caught and bought in the month besides some ducks and geese shot and shipped to St. Louis. At Cairo we shipped a cook and deck hand in the shape of an old colored man George Washington Davis, and his better two-thirds, Dinah, by name. They were darkies of "Anti-bellum" days, and had manners and graces that were truly Chesterfieldian, not arrogant and bigoted like the present generation. They wished to go to Vicksburg and were in no hurry and agreed to work their way. Uncle George was a tall, square built man of seventy-odd years; still straight as a cane and as active as a man half his age. In fact he would put all us boys to shame in following the dogs through swamps and brakes always jolly and full of fun and would take a joke in the same spirit it was given and would always spring one himself if opportunity offered.

Aunt Dinah, a good old soul, was as much too

fat as her spouse was too lean, and she stood more in the place of a mother to us wild "boys" than we realized until it came to parting. And what a cook! The writer has traveled a great deal and eaten all varieties of food, cooked in all styles, by all kinds of cooks, and would today pass them all up for just one good meal, cooked as only Aunt Dinah could cook it. Pray pardon the digression, for I can never think of my old friends without wanting the world to know of them.

We left Cairo on the morning of December 11, and went down about twelve miles to where a son of one of our crew lived and where Uncle George had his "bar" dogs. We arrived there early in the day and all enjoyed ourselves hunting squirrel on the edges of the timber near the corn fields. "Mose," Uncle George's son, said there were lots of coon in some swamps and bayous a mile or two to the south, and if we would like to take part in a darky coon hunt he would send his boy out and get the neighbors and dogs (this was a colored settlement) and all would meet at his cabin at dusk. We were agreeable, so at dark we put a few bottles of liquid refreshments in our pockets and went over to the cabin. Arriving there we saw by the light of a torch, a crowd of twelve or fifteen darkies and about four times that number of dogs of all colors and breeds, though hounds predominated. The darkies all had a nod and a smile for us strangers and for Uncle George, who was acquainted with all there. A few moments were spent chatting pleasantly and then with a loud whoopee or two by Uncle George and an answering chorus by all the dogs, the hunt was on. The dogs broke for the timber and we followed at our leisure. Soon, however, our pace was changed. A long-drawn bay, followed by a few short yaps, and Uncle George exclaimed, "Dar's Drum and Snuffles (two of his dogs); we's shore gwine to cotch one coon."

The woods were soon full of music and merrily the chase led us. Old Zip found too many dogs to shake off his trail and being hurried went up in a tree; the darkies were for building a fire and shining him, but Wyant soon cut that short by flashing our bullseye lantern. One young darkey, called Mack, climbed up the tree and shook his coonship out and he landed right in the center of a bunch of darkies and dogs. What a melee! What a racket! A mixture of snarls, growls and cuss words. Parks, Graves, Wyant and I nearly died laughing. The coon, however, was soon dispatched, a bottle passed around and to the hunt again. This time the dogs made a kill on the ground and we only got there in time to see the dogs take a farewell shake. Our next coon swam the bayou and several darkies waded it, got the coon and brought back the dogs. We worked down that side of the bayou, getting 5 coon and 2 opossum, then ferried across a few at a time in an old flat-bottomed scow and came back on the opposite side, getting six more coon and eight opossum in one persimmon grove. We passed out our last bottle, bid our friends goodnight and went back to the boat and to sleep. In the morning the writer and Uncle George went ashore and got the bar dawgs, three in number, and the writer bought four likely looking dogs for four dollars, which now made us sixteen dogs. We at once put them under the care of our deck hand, who at once made a large coop for them on the hurricane deck. At noon we cast off our lines and drifted down until nearly dark, then we made a landing on the Missouri side, not far above Belmont. That night we tried

Uncle George's dogs—a hound and two curs—and also my purchase—two spaniels and two curs—we had gotten into a good location and got 8 coon and 6 opossum. We stayed here four nights, getting 34 coon, 20 opossum and 2 mink. On the morning we left we cut a shell cottonwood, getting 11 coon, the largest haul we ever made from one tree.

We worked along down the river, Hickman, New Madrid, Tiptonville, Barfield, and Osceola were all passed within a day or two between, and on December 24th we landed at Memphis and proceeded to get our "fixins" for Christmas. Turkey, sweet taters, cranberries, mincemeat and a few other things were purchased and both our cook and steward (Graves promoted from chef) were soon busy preparing for the morrow's feast, while the captain, engineer, pilot and crew were also busy baling up pelts for shipment. From here we shipped 440 coon, 227 opossum, 29 mink and 2 otter, which with 22 green pelts on hand, made us 1601 skins caught and traded for in less than two months. So far our trip had been a success, both as a source of pleasure and of profit. Santa Claus made our boat a visit and among other things he brought Uncle George a double barrel breech loader and a supply of brass shells to take the place of his old musket, which by a little help from Parks fell overboard a day or two before and was lost. He brought a new black silk dress for Aunt Dinah, which gave her much joy and caused her to swear undying fealty to "her boys." Our dinner was a success and with Uncle George dressed in his "sto clo's" officiating as waiter, everything passed off smoothly. The old man entered into the spirit of the occasion and treated each one as though he were an honored guest of the "Old Massa" whom he served so faithfully befo' de wah, and he railed on imaginary nigga's who were slow with their work in the kitchen. We arrived at Vicksburg on March 8. There we made our last shipment of furs, and in footing up our statements found that we had handled a total of 5281 pieces of fur and that we had made very good money. We soon sold our boat and part of the dogs, the rest we gave to Uncle George. He and Aunt Dinah soon located on a truck patch near town, and we ramblers took a boat back to St. Louis. There we parted company, Graves and Parks going up the river to follow market fishing, and Wyant and I coming back to Colorado to fork the festive "broncho" and to rope and brand "dogies" for the 66 (sixty-six bar) outfit and to wait patiently for another trapping season.

CPSIA information can be obtained
at www.ICGtesting.com
Printed in the USA
LVHW100320011122
732074LV00004B/110